Praise for
Write Like You Mean It

Extremely well synthesized, clear, and intuitively organized. More than most guides, it practices what it preaches. Future writers would do well to start here.

Taylor Norman, Editorial Director of Neal Porter Books

Diana Pavlac Glyer has the know-how to turn raw ideas into written reality. In *Write Like You Mean It,* she imparts her years of expertise, helping writers find their own best practice to stay disciplined and see their projects through to the end.

Nilo Nathaniel Tayag, Program Manager,
Writing & Tutoring Centers, Azusa Pacific University

Write Like You Mean It renewed my excitement for writing in all its forms. Reading these accessible yet richly packed chapters, I found myself chuckling, feeling relief, jotting down notes to incorporate into my college composition classroom, and thinking often of my own fierce struggles with my dissertation over the last few years. I wish I had read this book earlier, just as a way to understand why hard things are hard, how different parts of the writing process differ in cadence and approach, and what to do at each juncture. I'm thankful to come across this book now and receive from its deep well of insight, history, strategy, and heart!

Libby Kao, English PhD Researcher & Instructor,
University of California, Berkeley

Drawing on hard-won wisdom and storied experience, with practical advice and an obvious affection for the reader, the authors, Diana Pavlac Glyer and Abigail Stone, offer a lively and generous "how-to" that is destined to become an indispensable companion and guide to anyone who loves to, and wants to write. Had I read this book thirty years ago, I would have written more, better, and more joyfully since. But having read it, I am eager to take up the pen again.

Steve Bell, Singer, Songwriter, & Storyteller

Abigail Stone has supported me from day one in my writing through her encouragement, deep knowledge of the publishing industry, and thoughtful manuscript feedback. She is a true champion for writers, and that same care is evident in *Write Like You Mean It*. The book is a trove of wisdom that guides you through the writing process as if you have a mentor by your side. Filled with insightful reflections and practical strategies, it helped me better understand and refine my own approach to writing. I'm grateful to have this book in my arsenal as I begin my next project. A must-have resource for writers now and for generations to come.

K. T. Jay, Author of *Inkbound Inheritance*

Write Like You Mean It is an inspirational, motivational, practical tool for writers, whether you're just getting started or have been writing since before you can remember. As a screenwriter and poet, writing is my life. And still, I found insight that I'm going to use. The "Airport Man?" I'm taking that. The concept of just sitting there, even if you don't get anything done, being better than not sitting there and missing when an idea comes… I needed to hear that. I highly recommend this book to anybody who wants to learn how to bring their idea to life; anybody who needs renewal from feeling burnt out; or anyone who is even just a little curious about what the writing process looks like. This book is a comprehensive, thoughtful, clear, and detailed take on what's needed to actually devote yourself to writing. Now I need to put down this pen and pick up another as I go to work on my script!

Nicola Pieper, Screenwriter

Writing advice typically comes in three forms: technical advice, philosophical musing, and experiential lore. Put another way, writers are told what they should do, how they should perceive doing it, and how to do it the way someone else did. *Write Like You Mean It* threads a tight needle by skillfully blending the three in actionable ways without sacrificing the most important advice. Writing is messy, but this book offers practical guidance for creating a process that best serves each writer, allowing them to celebrate their messes by turning them into manuscripts.

Michael Dean Clark, Author Essayist, & Award-Winning Journalist

Write Like You Mean It sets authors up for victory, from focus, to flow, to crossing the finish line. Perfect for any genre of writing, this book accelerates the writing process through perseverance, tenacity, and grit! As the title of this book suggests, writing is a calling and a valuable craft worth pouring into!

Alexis Leigh Regan, Poet & Founder of *Vessels of Light* Journal

As an author and book coach, I've had the privilege of partnering with Abigail Stone professionally and have seen firsthand her unwavering commitment to writers and their work. She is not only highly skilled but deeply invested in helping authors succeed. This book carries that same heart. What I most appreciate is its emphasis on momentum—freeing writers from the pressure of a perfect first draft and instead guiding them to prepare thoughtfully, draft boldly, and revise with courage. It is wise, practical, and empowering—a trusted companion for writers ready to bring their most meaningful work fully to life.

Licia Rester, Author, Book Coach,
and the Creator of the 6-Figure Book Business Program

Many writing books offer advice on specific aspects of the writing journey, but *Write Like You Mean It* takes you all the way from the beginning stages to the destination. I teach at many writers' conferences, and I am grateful to finally have a book like this to recommend. One strength of *Write Like You Mean It is* that it combines an overview of the writing process with guidance on more particular aspects of writing, from overcoming psychological barriers to making good punctuation choices. It instructs and inspires. Are you unsure what next steps you should take in your writing project, whether you have started it or not? This book will help.

Joseph Bentz, PhD,
Author of *A Son Comes Home* and *Nothing is Wasted*

Without Diana Pavlac Glyer's model of starting strong, maintaining momentum, and (finally) getting it done, I never would have begun, endured, or completed the writing process for my dissertation and first draft of a book I've tried to write for decades. Her consistent and practical wisdom urged me on week by week, word by word, and chapter by chapter. Her vision of what I could accomplish and what my writing could achieve filled me with exactly the kind of support that made the writing process not only incredibly effective but also altogether enjoyable. I owe her more than I can say!

Rev. Dr. Andrew Lazo, Author, Speaker,
and Co-host of the *Pints with Jack* Podcast

I grew up believing that the work had to be done alone to be great. As a former student of Dr. Glyer's, one of the most important things she taught me is that writing is, and always should be, collaborative. In that spirit, *Write Like You Mean It* is a community you can take with you.

Chock full of wisdom from two experts who not only know what they're talking about but who truly live it out, it's an excellent companion and guide for writers of all ages and stages who need to get their ideas off the ground and into the world.

Kathryn H. Ross, Author of *Black Was Not a Label*

Write Like You Mean It is not a read-it-and-then-shelf-it book. My colleague Abigail Stone has guided countless authors through development and revision, and anyone who has worked with her will recognize that hard-won knowledge baked into every page. After untangling the mystique of writing, the book delivers what you need to begin and what to reach for when you're rolling.

Deborah Froese, Author, Story Coach,
and Executive Editor of Indigo River Publishing

Write Like You Mean It offers aspiring writers a lifetime of learning from a sought-after speaker, a gifted, award-winning teacher, and, most assuredly, a fine writer. Diana Pavlac Glyer's love for the pleasures of the writing life is only exceeded by her love of equipping others to navigate the process from pre-writing to publication. There is no one better to demystify the process of finding your voice and enhancing your productivity.

David Weeks, PhD, APU Honors College

Few people understand the craft of writing—and the habits that sustain it—better than Diana Glyer. As a literature scholar and writing coach, she has helped many of our doctoral students at Northwind Seminary not only complete their work but also learn how to write like an Inkling—with clarity, imagination, and the romantic spirit. This book captures her gift for guiding writers to find their own distinctive creative and scholarly voice. This transformative guide will serve any serious writer well.

Rev. Dr. Michael J. Christensen, Author & Professor,
Northwind Seminary

A wonderful resource for students and professionals alike, *Write Like You Mean It* provides the necessary steps to achieving your writing dreams!

Kinley Hartz, College Senior

Write Like You Mean It offers you the voice of a wise teacher guiding you from years of experience and profound understanding of the processes by which we create with words. If you want someone to walk with you through the work of writing till you hold that work in your hands, *this* is the book you need.

Lancia E. Smith, Founder, Publisher of Cultivating Oaks Press
and Author of *Cultivating a Writer's Life*

The techniques I learned over the years in Dr. Glyer's graduate courses are distilled in this book. *Write Like You Mean It* is the fruit of decades of research, writing, and, most importantly, hands-on experience with authors like me. The approach is remarkably accessible to a vast audience; the book brims with examples, analogies, seasoned insights, personal anecdotes, and "magic tricks" of best practices that will equip the young scholar and the established author alike. At its core, this book is a roadmap that gives its reader confidence and hope to embark on the exciting journey of writing.

Duane Litz, Student Ministries Pastor
Granada Heights Friends Church

I don't know how I got through this whole book in two days, two sittings; I was just too hooked to stop reading. Glyer graces us with yet another masterpiece that turns the daunting writing process into an approach that is instantly accessible to anyone who seeks to tell their tale. It demystifies the art of being a writer through practical, contemporary methods of brainstorming, drafting, revising, proofreading, and publishing. *Write Like You Mean It* reveals the magic in the mundane.

Ashli Lomeli, Writing Professor & Dissertation Editor
California Lutheran University

Also by Diana Pavlac Glyer

Bandersnatch: C. S. Lewis, J. R. R. Tolkien, and the Creative Collaboration of the Inklings

The Company They Keep: C. S. Lewis and J. R. R. Tolkien as Writers in Community

Clay in the Potter's Hands: Recognizing the Extraordinary Work of God in Your Ordinary, Everyday Life

The Major and the Missionary: The Letters of Warren Hamilton Lewis and Blanche Biggs

Write Like You Mean It

Diana Pavlac Glyer & Abigail Stone

BP
BERRY POWELL PRESS

Write Like You Mean It: Start Strong, Maintain Momentum, and (Finally!) Get It Done

Printed in the United States of America.
First paperback edition 2026

Cover Design by Kay McConnaughey
Interior Design by Carolyn Rafferty and Kay McConnaughey

Published by Berry Powell Press
Glendora, California
www.berrypowellpress.com

ISBN: 978-1-957321-30-1 (Paperback)
ISBN: 978-1-957321-31-8 (e-book)
Library of Congress Control Number: 2026906925

To anyone anywhere who has ever thought,
"I want to write a book, but I don't know how."
Take heart. We wrote this book for you.

It is sometimes said that the major discoveries have already been made and that there is nothing important left to find. This attitude is altogether too pessimistic. There are plenty of ideas and plenty of things left to discover. The trick is to find the right path from one to the other.

John Vane

Contents

Authors' Note

Collaboration is like carbonation for fresh ideas. Working together bubbles up ideas you would not have come up with solo, which gets you further faster.
Caroline Ghosn

In the following chapters, you'll find a series of steps that, taken together, will illuminate the pathway from blank page to finished manuscript, whether you are working on a book or writing an article, essay, dissertation, report, research paper, or blog post. Each step includes practical advice and inspirational examples. Throughout the chapters, you'll also find a few "magic tricks," that is, simple and very specific writing techniques that provide enormous benefits.

Overall, the process described in these pages is not just the fruit of our experience. It is gleaned from what countless writers have discovered through trial and error. Whatever your genre—fiction, nonfiction, screenwriting, or poetry—you will find that the manageable steps of the Pathway Approach will lower stress, enhance productivity, and prepare you to produce the best writing you have ever done.

You'll notice that while Diana Pavlac Glyer and Abigail Stone are identified as co-authors, the voice throughout the text is singular. After much deliberation, we've decided to present this material from Diana's point of view. It's a clumsy solution to a vexing problem: When two people write a book together, it's distracting to keep switching back and forth from one person to the other. We chose to write in a single voice because this approach is less taxing for the reader. Be assured. This project has been a true collaboration, with each of us working hard to gather ideas, draft text, refine content, and polish the style. We sincerely hope that as a result, this book reflects the breadth and rich content that is possible when writers choose to collaborate.

One more thing: The stories we recount in these pages are composites. Names and other details have been changed. But the stories? The stories are true.

Becoming a productive writer takes a lifetime, and as you may have already guessed, it's less about the destination than it is about the journey. But a clear way to make progress step by step from a good idea to a great manuscript is here in your hands.

Foreword

The path to becoming a published writer is often called a journey. If we want to get mythical (and why shouldn't we?) it can even be a "hero's journey," though when I started out in this game I felt nothing like a hero. Yet looking back after 30 years as a published author, I can see many elements of myth along the way. One of these is the character known as the Mentor, who shows up in the dark world to give the hero much-needed guidance.

Like Yoda, or Haymitch, or Mr. Miyagi.

Or Johnny, the shoeshine guy in *Police Squad*. That was the TV show in the 1980s that starred Leslie Nielsen as Detective Frank Drebin, and which morphed into the *Naked Gun* movie franchise.

My favorite bit from that show was when Drebin, needing a lead, would sit down for a shine with Johnny and ask him what he'd heard on the street. At first, Johnny would say he didn't know anything. Then Drebin would slip him some dough. Johnny would proceed not only to give Drebin info about the case, but about everything under the sun, including the Brazilian rubber supply!

One time, after Drebin gets up, a priest sits down. He asks Johnny, "What do you know about life after death?"

"I wouldn't know anything about it," Johnny says.

The priest slips him a bill, and Johnny says, "You talking existential being or anthropomorphic deity?"

I've had many mentors over the years, mostly via books on the craft. My office shelf is packed with them, all lovingly highlighted. I'll often leaf through a favorite volume to review the lessons learned, the paths taken, the joys discovered.

And now the authors of this book have appeared to help you, no matter where you are in your journey. You can read it from start to finish, or dip into it for specific advice when you need it.

Think of it as your own personal shoeshine guy, only better because you don't have to fork over a bill every time you open it. A one-time purchase price is all it takes. And that is a great investment in your future as a writer.

James Scott Bell
Los Angeles, California
March 19, 2026

PART ONE
Start Strong

For all of us, before we set out on any journey, we need at least two things: (1) a compelling vision of our desired destination, and (2) a plan for how to get there.
John Mark Comer

Are you working on a novel? Thinking about a memoir? Wondering if you can write a book that conveys your expertise and shares it with a wider audience? Chances are that ideas and images have been bubbling up for some time.

Or maybe you are trying to make progress on a school assignment, like a research paper, master's thesis, or doctoral dissertation. If so, you are not starting from scratch. You've been reading, researching, and maybe even submitting and publishing for quite a while.

Here's the thing: The writing process doesn't start at the point when you actually sit down and start putting words on the page. It starts as you consider great ideas and open yourself to new possibilities. You try to picture what that final project will look like, you talk with friends and colleagues, you consider your calendar, you rearrange your workspace, and you gather new insights. These activities are often referred to as "prewriting," but that term can give the wrong impression. Every one of these activities is an essential step in the writing process. Prewriting is writing, and careful attention to prewriting is the secret to starting strong.

In PART ONE, we'll take a look at this first phase. We'll consider the faulty assumptions that delay, discourage, and threaten to derail us. Then we'll identify the habits that work best for you—habits that will pave your way to success. After considering who you are as a writer, we'll look at the four key questions you can use to analyze the task before you. These four questions apply to any project you can think of. We'll conclude PART ONE by focusing on how to enrich the content of what you are writing by gath-ering as much raw material as possible so you never run out of things to say.

Minimizing obstacles, refining your process, analyzing your specific task, and then gathering fresh content. That's the work of PART ONE. Let's get started.

Chapter 1
REFOCUS
Transform Your Writing

What is the world's best writing advice? There's a lot of it out there. Just this morning, Kurt Vonnegut's list of "16 Rules for Writing Fiction" popped up on my social media feed. Vonnegut has long been one of my favorite authors. I admire him enormously, and here, in part, is what he had to say:

- Every character should want something.
- Every sentence must do one of two things—reveal character or advance the action.
- Do not ramble.
- Sound like yourself.
- Say what you mean.

That is great advice! I've offered the same advice to students who have taken my writing classes and to writers I've coached through master's theses, short-story contests, and dissertations. In fact, I've written some of Vonnegut's rules on an index card and pinned it to the bulletin board above my desktop.

It's not only great advice from a great writer, but it also aligns with advice I've gotten from others. Annie Dillard is one of them. Here, in sum, are a few of her guidelines for how to write:

- You want vivid writing. How do we get vivid writing? Verbs, first. Did he run quickly or did he sprint? Did he walk slowly, or did he stroll or saunter?
- Don't tell the reader that someone was happy or sad. When you do that, the reader has nothing to see. She isn't angry… she throws his clothes out the window. Be *specific*.
- Don't use any extra words. A sentence is a machine; it has a job to do. An extra word in a sentence is like a sock in a machine.

I love her use of imagery, and I agree: Each sentence must do its job. This emphasis on strong syntax and lean prose is also the heart of these classic rules from Strunk and White:

- Use the active voice.
- Put statements in a positive form.
- Use definite, specific, concrete language.
- Omit needless words.
- Place the emphatic words of a sentence at the end.

William Zinsser continues the theme: "Don't hedge your prose with little timidities. Good writing is lean and confident."

So does Stephen King. In his masterful book *On Writing*, King tells writers to leave out the boring parts, stick to their authentic style, get to the point, be relatable, and write as truthfully as possible.

King's book *On Writing* is one of the very best books ever written about writing; another is *Bird by Bird* by Anne Lamott. She not only emphasizes the importance of clarity and honesty, but she also emphasizes heart: "You must risk placing real emotion at the center of your work. Write straight into the emotional center of things."

Here is even more great advice from great writers:

- "Never use two words when one will do."
  – Thomas Jefferson
- "Leave out the parts that people skip."
  – Elmore Leonard
- "When you catch an adjective, kill it." – Mark Twain

I especially love this famous bit of advice from Anton Chekhov, encouraging writers to use vibrant imagery to make their writing come alive: "Don't tell me the moon is shining; show me the glint of light on broken glass."

Just to make sure I covered all the bases as I wrote this chapter, I googled "How to Write Well." Here, quoting now, is what Google had to say:

- *Be clear*: Make sure your writing is clear and concise. State your intent or objective and include only necessary information.
- *Use active voice*: Make your writing more engaging and direct by using active voice, which includes a clear subject that acts.
- *Keep paragraphs short*: Break information into small chunks to make reading easier.
- *Avoid repetition*: While repetition can add emphasis, it can also make writing awkward and difficult to read.
- *Choose clear language*: When you can choose between being clear or clever, choose clarity.
- *Anticipate questions*: Consider the questions your readers might have and try to anticipate them.
- *Avoid filler words*: Eliminate filler words and phrases, and don't pad weak words with adverbs.
- *Consider viewpoint*: If you're writing a story, you can tell it from the point of view of different characters.

Hmmm. It turns out that even Google provided a viable list. Great advice abounds, so writers should be all set to fill their pages and get the work done. Or is there something else, something more?

Great Advice: But Is It Enough?

While there is more than enough advice available to those who want to increase their skills, many writers continue to struggle. All of this advice, whether it comes from Kurt Vonnegut, Thomas Jefferson, or Google itself, tells us *what* to write but not *how* to write.

Suggestions like "Have compelling characters," "Do not ramble," "Use active voice," and "Be clear" tell writers one thing: what their finished work should look like. This advice is all product-centered; in other words, it describes the finished text. To quote John Mark Comer, each of these important guidelines provides us with "a compelling vision of our destination."

But what about the journey? *How* do you create compelling characters? *How* can you edit material to eliminate rambling? Put heart into your writing? Or state your main point in a way that is clear and compelling?

In short: *How* are you supposed to make your way from blank page to finished manuscript?

Let's say you are working on a newsletter, a short story, or an article for a journal. Or perhaps you are facing a deadline for a report in the office, a doctoral dissertation, or a book report that's due this Friday. *What does it take to actually buckle down and get the thing written?*

How do you even start? How do you get a handle on the expectations of this particular project? How often should you write, and where? How do you press on when you feel tired or frustrated? Or when writer's block sets in with a vengeance? And what should you do when you have a full draft in hand, but you know in your heart of hearts that it is not as good as it can be?

You may have tried to put all this advice into practice but gotten frustrated. You shrugged and told yourself, *That's just the way things are right now: busy lives, endless demands, little free time.* Perhaps you have even been tempted to tell yourself, *Maybe I don't have the talent to write well.*

No one *wants* to work this way, but many find it hard to imagine an alternative. Time management, self-discipline, or dark self-doubt: Whatever seems to be the cause, you own it and then determine to do better next time.

But how are you just supposed to "do better next time" if your habits haven't changed?

From Product to Process

The first step toward starting the work you've longed to write is shifting your attention from *product* to *process*. In other words, focus less on the rules for good writing and more on the habits that get will get you there. Let me explain it this way. One of my friends is famous for baking a spectacular special-occasion cake called "Mrs. Appleyard's Chocolate Poem." Imagine that the next time Lauralee brings her famous cake to a party, I thank her, help myself to a slice, and then ask her how to make it.

She answers thoughtfully. "The chocolate flavor is very pronounced," she says. "And the texture is dense without being cloying. Since it is four layers high, the frosting needs to be somewhat dense, not too fluffy, or it won't have enough structural integrity." She concludes with, "Honestly, the real secret is balancing the richness of dark chocolate with just the right amount of sweetness."

Good advice from a great baker. But if that's all the direction I have, what are the chances that I could take her advice, go home, and bake that cake myself? There is nothing wrong with any of her observations, but there is so much more I need to know! What ingredients do I need to gather? How do I prepare the batter? What size and kind of cake pans do I need? What is the baking time and temperature? And how do I assemble and decorate the finished cake so that it looks as good as it tastes?

The fact is, unless you are already an expert in the field, it's virtually impossible to recreate it yourself by looking at the end product. Whether it's baking a cake or writing a novel, all creative endeavors involve a step-by-step process. A gardener needs more than a picture of a beautifully landscaped backyard to know where, how, and when to plant. A beginning guitarist needs more than a good-quality recording of a favorite song to learn the position of fingers and the progression of the chords. A young artist can admire a painting, but they will need detailed information about brush sizes, color combinations, types of paper, and canvas styles before they can develop the necessary skills to do the same.

We expect bakers, gardeners, musicians, and painters to follow a process. This is common knowledge for any art form, and yet we seem to believe that writing is somehow different. But writers need practical insight into the process, just like every other creative. What steps does an author go through? Which part gets written first? Do they work from an outline? Do they write more than one draft? How much gets discarded along the way? Did the story go the way they expected, or did the characters surprise and redirect them? Were beta readers helpful? Were there false starts? Setbacks? Delays?

We have all seen writing that is finished, polished, and published. But think about it: Very few people have ever been invited into the messy middle. If we were to watch an accomplished author at work, what would we see? What is it—exactly—that happens between the spark of an idea and the satisfaction of a completed manuscript?

If we want to become productive writers, knowing our goal will only take us so far, and if we hope to make progress on our own projects, we need a different kind of insight. We need to know where to start. We need a sense of the in-between steps. We need to recognize the progress markers that let us know whether we are moving forward or running in circles. We need to understand what the process looks like.

Each person's writing process is as unique as their fingerprint. However, across the span of authors, genres, time periods, and styles, we find a common set of components that anchor an effective process. In this book, we'll tackle these major components together to shape a writing process that works for you. Your personalized process will guide you if you are writing a book, but it also offers a way to think about the process you can use for anything you write.

As I describe each step, I will share what I've learned, both from my own writing and from teaching thousands of writers how to produce their best work. I'll show you where to start, what to do next, and how to make decisions when there are multiple paths to choose from. Rest assured, these components do not require inordinate talent, an English degree, or quitting your job to write full-time. They are available to anyone ready to form new habits, make the process their own, and get things done.

A Process that Helps, Not Hinders

A word of caution: A good creative process is not a formula, a blueprint, or a recipe. Yes, there are universal steps and principles we will move through. But unlike a recipe that requires the same ingredients, sequence, and temperature in every instance for every person, a good creative process is not one-size-fits-all. In fact, trying to make it one can become an obstacle in itself.

With that in mind, how do we ensure the components presented in this book become a process that helps rather than a structure that hinders? First and foremost, a good process is *personal*. There needs to be lots of room to develop a system that meets your unique creative style. Each of us has our own ways of discovering ideas and communicating them. For example, author Haruki Murakami's writing routine involves waking up at 4 a.m. every day, writing for five to six hours, running ten kilometers, reading, and then going to bed at 9 p.m. With fourteen novels, five short-story collections, and multiple international bestsellers under his belt, it's clear this routine works for him. How wonderful that he found it. But would his routine produce the same outcome for you? Maybe, or maybe not. We falter when we assume one person's way is the only way to be a "real writer." A process is *not* generic.

Not only that: A good process is *flexible*. The most effective writers do not rigidly stick to one system but constantly revise and reinvent it. They change their process to suit their life stage and adapt to the precise demands of the project they're working on. This requires reflection and self-awareness as you move through this pathway. When I was in college, I did all my writing after midnight, when the dorm was quiet, and my homework was done. Now, I prefer to start early in the morning. An effective process is *not* a law.

And here's the real test: A good process is *generative*. The suggestions in this book should serve as starting points, ideas to get you thinking, possibilities to lead you to your breakthrough. Let these guidelines spark your own insights and open new possibilities. These suggestions should also serve as a vocabulary to help you identify what worked in the past and what you need to be successful in the future. A process is *not* intended to be comprehensive.

Finally, a good writing process is *recursive*. Unlike baking, the writing process invites you to loop back to revisit and refine earlier stages or leap forward, following your creative flow. In fact, a recursive process celebrates all the stopping, reflecting, erasing, regrouping, reorganizing, and rewriting. Those detours and hiccups,

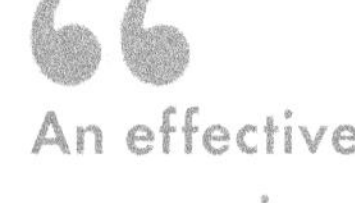

An effective writing process is personal, flexible, generative, and recursive.

delays and imperfections enrich the end product tenfold. They are part of the secret of getting to the good stuff. As creativity expert Mihaly Csikszentmihalyi says, "How many iterations it goes through, how many loops are involved, how many insights are needed, depends on the depth and breadth of the issues dealt with."

Hang on tight to this idea of looping back to an earlier stage or leaping forward to a later one. In many ways, the steps of the process are more like loops in a coil rather than a straightforward progression. We'll talk about each step one at a time, but each of your projects will progress according to its own pattern. The process is *not* linear.

MAGIC TRICK
Borrow From the Best

No doubt you've already read any number of books about writing. While many of them focus on rules that govern the final product, others offer a window into the writer's actual practice as they cultivate a writer's life. As mentioned, Stephen King's *On Writing* and Anne Lamott's *Bird by Bird* are particularly helpful. Other works offer insight into the processes used by writers from the past: John Steinbeck, for example, kept a diary as he wrote *The Grapes of Wrath*, and it has been published as *Working Days*. If you want to do a really deep dive into the habits of acclaimed writers, there is no better source than *The Paris Review* interviews. They include sixty years of in-depth interviews with prominent writers, all focusing on their daily habits.

Take a little time to search for information about your favorite authors, the ones you return to again and again. Focus not so much on what they have written but on *how* they got it done. Did they type it out or write it longhand? Do they work best in a noisy coffee shop, a silent library, or a well-equipped home office? Are there accountability tricks they use to help them stay focused and on track? How do they handle it when inspiration vanishes and deadlines loom?

Even better, you may know an experienced writer who is just a phone call away or two doors down the hall. Reach out to a friend or colleague who has made good progress in the writing life. Sit down for a cup of coffee, ask questions, compare notes, and learn all you can about how they do what they do.

Want to turn all this good information into magic? Choose a few writing habits that most intrigue you, and try them for yourself. If they don't work, try something else; if they help, keep them and build on them. You might be surprised to find what fits.

Will This Book Help You Become a Better Writer?

All this talk about the writing process is great, but will this book really help you become a better writer? The answer is a resounding yes. When we momentarily release the goal and focus on the steps toward it, we're not only more likely to reach it; the work we produce will be so much better. It's more thoughtful, nuanced, creative, and original. You don't just finish the work—you finish your best work.

Write Like You Mean It is the essential guidebook for writers who are ready to cultivate the habits that consistently produce strong writing. It provides a specific and practical pathway that will take you from scribbled notes—on your phone, laptop, Moleskine journal, or 8 ½ x 11-inch yellow pad—to a completed draft, and then to a polished one. It approaches an old, familiar topic by shifting your focus away from the words on the page and inviting you to consider the actions, decisions, tools, and perspectives you use as you write.

If you're ready to improve what you write, the next chapter will help you discover your path through the creative process.

Chapter 1 Summary
REFOCUS

- Much of the available writing advice focuses on the characteristics of good writing.
- Becoming better writers requires more: It means rethinking *how* we write.
- We can learn a lot by examining the process used by successful writers.
- An effective writing process is personal, flexible, generative, and recursive.

The Big Idea
To improve your product, focus on improving your writing process.

Take a Step
Think back to a writing project that went well, one that you are proud of. What two or three aspects of your process contributed most to your success?

A Final Word
Even small changes to your writing process will yield remarkable results and ensure that, this time, you will not only complete that project but also be more satisfied with the work you have done.

Chapter 2
DISCOVER
Find Your Path

I wrote my first novel in fourth grade. I was in that phase when all I could think about were horses, and the only author I read was Marguerite Henry: *Misty of Chincoteague*, *King of the Wind*, *Justin Morgan Had a Horse*, *Black Gold*, and *Sea Star*. When I had exhausted every story Henry had written, I found more: *Black Beauty*, *National Velvet*, *My Friend Flicka*. Then my local library ran out of books about horses, and I couldn't find more of what I wanted to read, so I figured I'd have to write some myself.

I had just finished reading *Blitz: The Story of a Horse* by Hetty Burlingame Beatty, so I decided to call my book *Blaze: The Story of a Horse*. I don't remember much about it, except that Blaze was a wild horse who was captured and tamed by a nine-year-old girl. Blaze was trained to pull an old-fashioned fire truck and, in the end, saved a family from a house fire just in time.

As I think about that novel now, I am thankful that I was able to channel my love for horses into a creative piece of my own, derivative as it was. I didn't know it back then, but I'd already tapped into my love for making sense of my world through writing—and a desire to communicate through the written word.

The Panic Pattern That Keeps Writers Stuck

Watch young children play and create, and you'll notice that they haven't learned to be self-conscious. They move naturally to music, or sing with abandon, or draw whatever they want using any color they choose. They dive in, lose track of time, and explore without overthinking. They delight in making things and are proud to share their creations with others. Completely free from self-conscious distraction, they plunge into the flow of the creative process, at one with the experience.

Unfortunately, this creative freedom can be difficult to access when we sit down to write. For many writers, the natural ease of writing has faded away. As a teacher, I see how torturous writing assignments can be for my students. Without that child-like courage to compel them, and without a clear writing process to lean on, they fall prey to what I call the Panic Pattern:

Step 1: Receive an assignment and due date.
Step 2: Wait for motivation and inspiration to arise.
Step 3: Panic when the words won't come.
Step 4: Procrastinate and feel terrible about it.
Step 5: Write something (anything) at the last minute.
Step 6: Turn it in.
Step 7: Decide they never want to write anything ever again.

I want to say this pattern only applies to students, but to be honest, I've been there too. If I sit around and wait for the perfect words to somehow present themselves, I'll panic, procrastinate, and, inevitably, run out of time. And then? I'll create a piece of writing that I'm not proud of. From my work with other writers, I know I'm not alone. This pattern plagues journalists, bloggers, and professional writers, too.

Some writers are working under the pressure of an externally imposed deadline. But others are trying to establish a habit of posting on social media or exploring a book idea on their own time. They often follow their own kind of Panic Pattern:

Step 1: Get an idea for a writing project.
Step 2: Write a bunch of stuff.
Step 3: Get stuck, run out of ideas, or decide it isn't very good.
Step 4: Wait around for motivation and inspiration.
Step 4: Panic when the words won't come.
Step 6: Give up altogether and let the idea die.

Think of all the books, poems, essays, dissertations, stories, and songs that never made it through the throes of the Panic Pattern. How many times have you started full of hope, then given up in frustration and despair? How many times have you asked yourself, "Why can't I get the thing written?" Let's break the pattern by unpacking what stands between these Panic Patterns and an effective writing process.

What Stands in Your Way?

What is most remarkable about the childlike experience of creative play is that while in this state, it never occurs to us that we are limited. There are no rules. No finish lines. No row of judges ready and waiting to hold up signs to evaluate our performance. What changes? Why do so many come to dread the blank page? Why do so many talented writers fail to reach their potential?

Receiving Criticism Instead of Guidance

As we grow up, that pure, unbridled desire to express ourselves creatively gets hampered by negative feedback. In school, a teacher's red pen or scathing words may have dashed every hope. When others highlight errors rather than courage, conviction, and exploration, it can send you and your imagination into hiding.

As children, we can't control this outside criticism. But as adults, we find ways to shield ourselves from destructive voices.

Getting Stuck on Imaginary Rules

We all make assumptions about what we are and are not allowed to do when we write, and imaginary rules often box us in. For example, have you ever believed any of the following statements?

- I need to know exactly what I'm going to write before I write it.
- I have to start writing at the beginning.
- I can't write the next section until I finish the one I'm working on.
- "Writing time" means sitting at a desk and drafting text.
- If I spent time writing it, I have to keep it.
- Real writers write early in the morning.
- I have to start with an outline.
- I have to finish a full draft before I get feedback.

Odds are, you've believed at least one of these, at least subconsciously. Maybe you internalized imaginary rules from a former teacher or a portrayal of a writer you saw on TV. Some may be helpful—maybe you do benefit from writing at the crack of dawn or outlining first. Yet not one of these rules is inherently true. These "rules" may very well contradict what works for your own creative process.

The truth? Real writers take the time to figure out what works for them. As you think about your writing process, notice any imaginary rules that come up for you. Ask: "Is this a rule that's helping me make progress toward my writing goals?" If not, discard it or adapt it and press on.

Being Stifled by External Requirements

While you might have an innate attraction to writing, the joy may have been lost because you've been forced to write a certain way, whether you want to or not. Teachers can assign written assignments on topics that do not interest you or push you to follow a format that feels awkward and unnatural to your writing sensitivities.

Work assignments may also dampen our vision. While you have a desire to put your ideas into words, this creative need isn't met by writing a grant proposal or drafting an annual report. Writing can become a dry and arduous task. The delight of childhood creativity can fade into the background.

But now, you have a fresh opportunity to choose projects of your own. You can develop and refine a process that engages your personality and reflects the realities of this stage in your life.

Lacking Guidance About the Writing Process

Perhaps the most significant reason writers don't reach their potential is that quality writing instruction is not always available in our education system. We're somehow supposed to know how to produce words, paragraphs, and pages in a way that connects with others. Without a clear direction that guides you as you develop an effective writing process, what can you do? Through trial and error, you make up rules for yourself and cling tightly to each one, whether or not these guidelines have produced good results.

How Real Writers Write

When I taught high school, I would often give short in-class writing assignments to focus students' attention, check their reading comprehension, or prepare them for class discussion. I would write along with them. Some days, I'd sit at my desk;

other times, I'd use an overhead projector or write my brief essay on the chalkboard.

I remember one eleventh-grade class in particular. As they settled in, I asked them to write a quick essay about a time they did something courageous. They chatted for a few moments, gathered paper and pen, and then started to write. I turned to the whiteboard, listed a few initial ideas, and then began drafting a few paragraphs of my own. After a few minutes, I became aware that the usual friendly banter and shuffle of papers had been replaced with utter silence.

I turned around to see every single pair of eyes locked on me. "What's the matter?"

No answer.

"Why are you watching me instead of writing your essays?"

I wondered if they were scanning my work to see if somehow I had given away the "right answer" to the day's writing prompt.

There was a pause, and then a strong, brave voice came from the back row.

"Dr. Glyer," he said, "Umm, you're not a very good writer."

"Really? Why do you say so?"

"Well, you keep stopping and staring off into space instead of writing stuff. And you keep erasing what you wrote and then writing it some different way all over again."

I realized then that they were watching me because they'd never seen someone write in public before. Writing is often a private, secret, almost magical act. For the very first time, they were invited to watch someone actively engaged in the writing process—and it was not at all what they expected. I spent more time thinking than writing. I tried out various wordings and then erased it and tried again. My words did not unfold in a smooth, seamless, linear sequence.

Time after time, in the classroom, at conferences, in workshops and seminars, when I write in public, those around me stop what they are doing and stare at me as I write.

What fascinates me most about this is what it reveals about the way we view the writing process. Most people assume that good writers know what they want to say before they write the first sentence. Some have been told as much: "Know what you want to say and then say it." But if, instead, you need to stop, think, start, and restart multiple times, people assume you are a bad writer.

It's not just students who hold this erroneous belief; nearly every beginning writer I have ever known has held this misconception to some degree.

And not only that: Most of the experienced writers I know are praying for the day when the writing process stops being so messy and complicated and the words flow easily, effortlessly, page after page after page.

The truth? It's the stopping, the thinking, reconsidering, and discovering, the starting and restarting, over and over again, that make the masterpieces we know and love. And the process tends to get *less* tidy, not more seamless, the longer we practice our craft.

How have so many of us become so misled as to what makes good writing? Writer and professor Joseph Harris says, "This one-draft view of writing is reinforced by most movie and TV depictions of writers at work, as we watch them quickly type perfectly balanced and sequenced sentences until, with a sigh of satisfaction, they pound out THE END or press SEND." In the absence of any real models, it makes sense to rely on these faulty media representations.

Here is the most treacherous part of the portrayal we see in the media. When we believe "good writers" produce gorgeous prose in one shot every time, we elevate good writing to an absolutely unattainable standard. So it's total self-sabotage to hold ourselves to such an unrealistic model.

With this flawed idea of the writing process, *we* are the ones telling ourselves, "You keep stopping, erasing, and starting over again. You must not be a very good writer." If we can never measure up to our own standards, why keep going? The truth is, most don't.

MAGIC TRICK

Excavate the Past

For better or worse, our creative impulse is impacted by the voices that surround us. Parents, teachers, friends, colleagues. Things we've seen on TV or read in books. Rejection letters from publishers, or that one time when we failed to make the cut in a contest, an exhibit, or the school's literary magazine. One or two of these can sow the seeds of doubt. A handful? Enough to shut us down entirely.

How do we break free from these voices from the past? We start by recognizing them. Spend a little time reflecting: Who has given you feedback on your writing or criticized your creative projects? Has negativity and discouragement taken root? Has a casual comment solidified into a foundational assumption? When you try to move forward, are you haunted by doubts from the past? Perhaps you are ready to enter a new season, one where you can acknowledge the damage done and put an end to its poisonous effects.

How do we find the courage to move forward and start making real progress? Bad memories may have wounded us; good memories may aid us here. Who have been your greatest allies as you have exercised your creative gifts? One of my friends loves to talk about a neighbor who bought her a first set of watercolors. Another shares about a Christmas when her parents presented her with her very own guitar. One of my friends recently posted this tribute on Facebook: "When I was a kid, I told my aunt that I wanted to fly, and she believed me. In high school, she told me I had a future even though I couldn't see past graduation. I went to college, and she was the one who believed I could go to the places that others said were out of reach for a kid like me. When I became a parent, she believed I could create the home life that I was never afforded. And now, as a leader, storyteller, producer, and artist, she still believes in me. She still loves me and believes in my dreams."

Who is that person in your life who believes you can do anything, go anywhere, and accomplish things that have never been done before? Was there a teacher who told you that you had a talent? Is there someone who equipped you with creative materials—a used laptop, perhaps, or a beautiful leather-bound journal? Is there a friend or family member who was deeply moved by something you wrote? Who believes in you still?

Pause to identify old wounds and relinquish them. Take time to remember faithful advocates and thank them. This process can be a powerful, almost magical step as we lay the foundation for building new habits.

The Pathway Approach

Obviously, the Panic Pattern is not an effective process—new and seasoned writers alike know this all too well. But most just haven't caught a vision for any other way. Writers who complete the journey from blank page to final draft generally develop their unique version of these nine stages.

Define Your Task: Identify the scope of your project.
Stockpile Ideas: Gather an abundance of material, insights, and details.
Honor Your Workstyle: Choose the best time and place to write.
Write Fast: Produce a really rough first draft.
Overcome Obstacles: Defeat discouragement, distraction, and overwhelm.

Rework the Big Picture: Revise your content and strengthen your structure.
Refine Your Style: Hone your voice, improve the flow, and add finesse.
Fix Mistakes: Identify and eliminate distracting errors.
Reach Your Readers: Understand options for sharing your work.

The stages listed above summarize the Pathway Approach—a concrete yet adaptable set of steps from start to finish. This is the pathway we will travel together in the pages to come.

Panic or Pathway: What's the Difference?

There are many key differences between the Panic Pattern and the Pathway Approach. For one thing, writers who fall back into the Panic Pattern spend most of their time waiting for inspiration to strike and then labor to get every word exactly right the first time through.

On the other hand, those who practice the Pathway Approach spend a lot of their time preparing. They take time to plan their process, think through the nature of their task, and gather essential content. Next, they create really rough drafts really quickly. And after that, they patiently rework and improve what they have written.

I like to invoke what I call "The 50-20-30 Rule for Writers." Writers who follow the Panic Pattern spend nearly 100% of their time focused on producing a single, polished draft. On the other hand, writers who follow the Pathway Approach spend 50% of their time and energy *preparing*, about 20% of their time *drafting*, then they rest, regroup, and devote the remaining 30% of their time and attention to fearless *revising*. The proportions may vary, but the principle remains the same: They spend less time drafting and much more time prewriting and rewriting.

An effective writer's process lowers stress by acknowledging that writing is not a one-and-done achievement but a process managed page after page through a flexible, recursive workflow. But there is an even greater difference between these two processes, and that is the quality of the writing they produce. The Panic Pattern produces writing that tends to be unfocused, underdeveloped, disorganized, and most significantly, *unoriginal*. Without taking the time to really develop our unique perspective, we often write top-of-the-head, predictable prose that restates something someone else has already said better. That unique, creative voice fails to come through, leaving both you and your reader dissatisfied.

In the pages that follow, we'll take a deep dive into each step of the Pathway Approach. As you learn the tasks that are to be completed in each step, you will use this knowledge to develop your own effective writing process, one that is personal, flexible, and generative. As you consider the advice in these pages, discard what doesn't work for you and be willing to experiment with new possibilities. Stay nimble and constantly adapt. Through core concepts, clear examples, personal encouragement, and inspiration, we'll demystify the writing process and leave you with a new framework—and a lot of specific, practical tips—for (finally!) completing your writing task.

> "
> The 50-20-30 Rule for Writers: 50% preparing, 20% drafting, 30% fearless revising.

Chapter 2 Summary
DISCOVER

- Many writers operate in a pattern characterized by waiting for inspiration, panicking when it doesn't come, and giving up.
- Even the most talented writers can become discouraged by criticism or constrained by rigid, artificial expectations.
- Since we rarely get to observe someone in the process of writing, many believe the myth that good writing comes out perfect the first time.
- One way to renew our hope is to remember the people who have equipped and encouraged us.
- There is a pathway forward: take plenty of time to prepare, produce a really rough first draft, then patiently rework what you have written.

The Big Idea

When you commit to spending more of your time preparing to write and then revising what you have written, the process is less stressful, and the result is richer and more refined.

Take a Step

Are there rules you have been told or habits you have adopted that have stood in the way every time you try to write? Identify them and move on.

A Final Word

Instead of panicking and procrastinating, you can develop a flexible writing process that empowers you to make steady progress through any writing task.

Chapter 3
ANALYZE
Define Your Task

Wherever you are in the writing process, it is all too easy to become overwhelmed. The Pathway Approach provides the missing map through this fog of uncertainty. The first step is to define your task and understand the constraints and opportunities inherent in different kinds of writing projects. This is an essential aspect of prewriting, the careful preparation that is the key to success. As Gordon B. Hinckley has observed, "Preparation precedes power."

Let me introduce the topic this way. When I give my students a writing assignment, most of them are quick to ask two basic questions: "How long does my paper need to be?" and "When is it due?"

While this is vital information, my most savvy students will dig much deeper, asking questions that get at the foundation of the assignment. Naturally, they start by tailoring their paper to the teacher's demands. Is she a stickler for grammar? Does she allow personal stories? Is she picky about page length? They might ask questions like, "Should the essay just summarize the book's main points or is it supposed to be arguing for something?" or "Who should we assume the reader is? How much do they already know?" While issues like word count are important, they recognize that a beautifully written descriptive essay won't get many points if it is supposed to present a researched argument, even if it is turned in on time.

These students intuit a key principle that applies to all writers: Each piece of writing is a unique task with particular demands.

Four Key Questions

Before skilled writers begin their work, they interrogate the assignment, taking time to analyze the work's purpose, the needs of their audience, the genre, and the message to be conveyed. Writing is communication. That's why writing is considered strong and compelling when it suits the situation. As my mentor Donald M. Murray used to remind us in class, "There is no such thing as good writing. There is only appropriate writing."

Four key questions inform appropriate writing:

1. Purpose: Why am I writing this? What is my ultimate goal?
2. Genre: What type of document am I creating? What are the defining characteristics?
3. Message: What is the bottom line? What am I really trying to say?
4. Audience: Who will be reading it? How do I meet their needs and expectations?

What Is Your Purpose?

From a big-picture perspective, the most basic question is *why.* "What is my goal in writing this project?" The project must fulfill a purpose, or why bother with writing it at all?

The answer could be that you want to write solely for your own amusement or personal growth. Journaling and other forms of self-exploratory writing can be an end in themselves. After all, writing is one of the most effective ways we can learn about ourselves. It allows us to put feelings and thoughts onto a page where we can observe them. Over time, we can revisit our words and see how or if we've changed. Perhaps it is a way to express our creativity by telling a story, inventing characters, or describing an image I see. Or perhaps this piece serves as an experiment that will help me practice my style or strengthen specific skills? Will it help me process a complicated experience, or gain clarity about an event, or remember the details of a specific situation, or get in touch with a vague emotion?

In addition to the internal reasons, we also write to reach others: to share a practical tip, offer a new perspective, or seek a response, such as requesting a refund from an airline.

Even when you are just tinkering with an idea for a poem, play, novel, or short story, reflecting on your purpose can make a powerful difference. For example, if you are writing a series of mystery novels with the primary goal of financial success, you will make different decisions than if your deeper purpose is to use those stories to address a social problem, highlight an underrepresented identity, or explore an unusual subculture.

There are so many reasons to write.

- I want to publish a book that will share my expertise and help build my business.
- I want to share my story to help and inspire those who are going through similar challenges.
- I am earning my degree, and I need to get a good grade on this term paper.
- Writing a monthly report is required by my job, and I want to satisfy my superiors.
- I'd like to publish this article in a magazine.
- I have an idea for a poem, and I want to see if I can pull it off.
- I want to document my family history or explain life lessons I have learned.

Clarifying your purpose in writing creates a center of gravity for all future decisions—editorial or otherwise. Your purpose determines what you will choose to include and how you will express it. And your purpose is ultimately the measuring stick that will tell you whether the work you created missed the mark or achieved what you intended.

What Is Your Genre?

Beyond purpose, another foundational question is genre, the types or categories of writing. Consider a simple example: a handwritten letter from a friend. You expect to see a salutation, such as "Dear [Name]." You expect to see a sign-off, like "Sincerely Yours." And then you expect to see their signature.

However, you have no such expectations when you receive a text message from the same person. In fact, a text that contained a salutation and a sign-off, or even punctuation for that matter, would not only be awkward but might actually be offensive. A handwritten letter and a text message are two different genres.

Each genre has its own peculiar set of expectations. Think about the inherent elements we look for in a fantasy series, for example, or a romance novel, a cozy mystery, or a science fiction story. Or consider the shape of different forms of written text: a play script, a Shakespearean sonnet, or a nature documentary. There are dozens of genres, and each has a host of specific, non-negotiable expectations built into it.

Even in a given field, say journalism, there are many different genres, such as breaking news, investigative reporting, and sports coverage, and each has its own rules. When I worked as a journalist, I wrote concert reviews and feature stories. I needed to make sure each piece met the expectations of my editor, my readers, and my publication. These external factors determined the length and amount of detail, the focus, and the tone.

Perhaps you remember an English class where some writing assignments were informative summaries, while others were analytical or argumentative. If you are writing for an assignment, it is important to clarify the genre with the person who gave you the prompt.

Once you have identified your genre, how do you learn the rules? Stephen King is emphatic about the two necessary components: "If you want to be a writer, you must do two things above all others: read a lot and write a lot. There's no way around these two things that I'm aware of, no shortcut." King believes it, and he practices what he preaches. "I'm a slow reader," he says, "but I usually get through seventy or eighty books a year, mostly fiction." By immersing himself in the genre he likes best, he absorbs thousands of insights, some consciously and some not. He learns style, pacing, voice, and structure. He notices characters, settings, and the fine art of plot points. "Every book you pick up has its own lesson or lessons," he says, "and quite often the bad books have more to teach than the good ones."

This principle—read a lot—is evident in the lives of every experienced writer that I know. When my coauthor, Abigail, is working on a book, she checks out a stack of similar books from the library. Abigail skims them looking for patterns in tone, density, chapter length, and so on, all to get a sense of what readers of that genre have come to expect. My friend Tom is writing a memoir. So he spends a lot of his prewriting time reading memoirs, deliberately choosing books and authors that represent a wide variety of topics, time periods, situations, personalities, and styles. Another friend is working on a self-help book. He heads down to Barnes & Noble and examines the very shelf where he hopes he will find his own book someday. Then he does a deep dive into the pages of the best-selling self-help books to see how they approach their message.

Read a lot and read widely. You will learn an enormous amount about genre simply by immersing yourself in published texts. As your writing projects are taking shape, keep the key components of the genre in mind. Which structures should you attend to? What tone, pacing, and tropes appear again and again? Where should you incorporate these same features, and where should you innovate, adding your unique voice to this established tradition?

What Is Your Message?

When you think about movies you love and novels you read, you'll notice that underneath the characters and plot, there is often a deeper message. Often, the theme is hinted at or explored through character, dialogue, or situation. But sometimes the theme is stated explicitly. In Peter Jackson's film *The Hobbit: An Unexpected Journey*, Gandalf says, "Some believe that it is only great power that can hold evil in check. But that is not what I have found. I have found it is the small things. Every day deeds of ordinary folk that keep the darkness at bay. Simple acts of kindness and love." This is the theme, and it is played out in scene after scene of the film.

All good communication has a message. Think about how frustrating it is when a friend sits down to tell you a story and, instead of getting to the point, they present you with a whole series of unrelated events. "You know that new gas station over on Bennett Avenue? I stopped there yesterday, and I ran into Paul. I haven't seen him in at least a decade. We used to be part of the same hockey team. He's been super excited about that last game with Connor McDavid. I had a friend named Connor when I was in grade school. Our teacher back then was Ms. O'Reilly. I totally loved the way she taught statistics. It wasn't her specialty, but she just loved to tie stuff together with stuff that happened in the past, like, a long time ago. I'm a big fan of the History Channel, and I watch those shows all the time." And on and on. And on.

As you are working to find your message, it helps to distinguish between your message and your topic. A topic might be something like this:

Travel
Farming

Raising toddlers
Watercolor painting
Computers

When I push my students to lean into their topic and find their message, they usually narrow down their topic and give me something like this:

Travel tips for seniors
Farming the old-fashioned way
Single parents who are raising toddlers
The joy of watercolor painting

That's better. But it still doesn't tell me what they will claim, argue, describe, or explain *about* their topic. They've just made their topic more specific. So how do you move from topic to message? Tell your reader what they will discover as they read your work. Here are some examples of how the specific topics I listed above could be expanded into a specific message:

Travel may present some specific challenges for older adults, but there are many ways to make the journey simpler and more enjoyable.

Although technology has changed the face of **farming**, there are ten old-fashioned, time-tested techniques that remain invaluable.

Single parents need to prioritize their own healthy patterns if they hope to keep pace with energetic toddlers.

Traditional **watercolor painting** is hard to master, so more and more beginning artists are exploring loose, abstract approaches to their work.

I am a great fan of musicals, and one of my all-time favorites is *Hamilton.* The topic of that play is the founding of America. But in many ways, the play is really about legacy. Alexander Hamilton asks, "What is a legacy? It's planting seeds in a garden you never get to see. I wrote some notes at the beginning of a song someone will sing for me." That question haunts Alexander Hamilton, and it animates the whole story.

We must consider the meaning behind whatever we are writing—what deeper thread will animate our work? Is our message meant to offer a specific insight, correct a misconception, argue a controversial point of view, issue a call to action, or amuse and entertain?

If we plan to publish our work, whether that means a contract with a major publishing house or a post on social media, we'll also want to consider how our message contributes to the conversation. For our writing to get noticed, we'll want to offer something new—"Not enough people are talking about this," and different—"Here's a perspective I'm not seeing." Our message defines what conversations we are entering and what we will say when the floor is ours.

Who Is Your Audience?

Novice writers who want to gain the largest readership possible may be tempted to imagine "a general audience," you know, a generic, vague, all-purpose reader. They figure the more people they try to reach, the more copies of their book they will sell. But writing is, in essence, a conversation, a social act with a strong sense of connection between the authors and their readers. Generic writing rarely hits home. It is the writer's responsibility to discern and adapt to readers' needs. What engages one group is certain to bore or alienate another.

Audience determines the content. The information I share, the amount of explanation needed, and the clarity of definitions will vary from one audience to another. The examples I select must resonate with the specific individuals I hope to reach.

The audience also impacts my tone. The person you are trying to reach will determine not only what you say but how you say it. When I speak to my eight-year-old daughter, I use a different tone than when I speak to my boss, my pastor, or my best friend. My voice may be stern, cheerful, desperate, or exasperated. My mood may be brusque, irritable, hopeful, encouraging, urgent, or affectionate. My role may be instructive, confrontational, or winsome. My approach may be direct or indirect, heavy-handed or lighthearted. It is these particularities of voice that make writing come alive.

So I need to know my readers. Do they share a specific interest, speak a particular jargon, hold certain values, or congregate in a common location? Answering questions like these and many more will guide the decisions I make, suggesting what to avoid, what to include, and how best to convey my message.

There is a quick in-class exercise that I like to do with my college students to underscore the power of knowing your audience. It works best on a Monday, sometime in the morning, and early in the semester.

As students arrive in the classroom, we chat about their weekend: "How did it go? What did you do?" Then I ask them to answer those same questions in an ungraded, in-class writing assignment, encouraging them to write quickly and do so in four very different ways:

- As a text to your best friend from high school
- As a letter to your priest, rabbi, or other religious acquaintance
- As dialogue, such as a quick phone call to your mom, aunt, or other trusted family member
- As a five-paragraph essay (intro, three points, and a conclusion) for a grumpy, exacting, demanding English teacher

My students love it. They dive in, and they really ham it up. It's fun for them to write about such an easy topic, and they like playing around with different approaches to telling the same story.

I put them in groups of three and have them read aloud from their essays. And then we talk about their work.

Were there differences in your content? Did you include some details in sharing with one person that you left out when talking to the others?

How about sentences? Did you even use complete sentences? Did you think about subject-verb agreement, or double-check your spelling?

How formal or elevated was your tone? Would you describe it as blue jeans, a tuxedo, or a simple coat and tie? How much warmth and familiarity did you include? Or did you keep it impersonal, distant, and strictly factual?

Did your use of structural clues like sequence, paragraphing, introduction, and conclusion change from one piece of writing to another?

What about the purpose in each case: To entertain? Persuade? Inform? Connect?

My students learn that they use different words, different sentence structures, different tone, and, frankly, entirely different content. They also discover that they are, in fact, very good at adapting their writing to various audiences. They instinctively use longer and more complex sentences when writing for an English teacher. They use shorthand and jargon when talking with a peer. Their tone changes when they are sharing an experience versus asking for a favor, trying to impress, or asking a serious question.

This ability to adapt the way we communicate is called "code shifting." We all do it, and most of us can do it effortlessly. The way you talk to a stranger while waiting in line at the coffee shop is different from the way you talk with someone you've known since grade school (relationship). The way you address a teacher or a person in authority is different from the way you talk with a peer (formality). The mood and circumstances will affect how concerned you are about correctness (situation).

Another thing my students learn from this exercise is that each one of the approaches they adopt still reflects their authentic self. They are who they are, even as they modify how they communicate. I encourage them to expand their range and learn to deliberately shift their style, making countless adjustments to the constraints and the opportunities of each rhetorical situation.

MAGIC TRICK

A Reader Archetype

When I was working on my book *Bandersnatch*, I wanted to write to an audience that wasn't steeped in academia. But I had a hard time leaving my academic and professorial voice behind. I kept sliding back into arguing, overexplaining, and using way too much jargon.

The fix? I invented my ideal reader. I called him "Airport Man," and I imagined a businessman wandering around LAX waiting for his flight to New York. He's looking for a good book to keep him occupied on the long flight. Fiction is okay, but he's hoping to learn something new. He grabs a copy of *Bandersnatch*. "This looks different," he thinks. "This might be good."

Airport Man was a reader archetype: a person, real or imaginary, who encapsulated qualities of my ideal reader. Picturing Airport Man changed how I wrote *Bandersnatch*, and it gave me much-needed guidance not only as I wrote the book, but also as I worked with an illustrator. It brought clarity and focus. It changed my tone, word choice, and content. It was magic.

Here's the most important gift that I received from Airport Man: Picturing him helped me cut out a whole lot of material that was super interesting to me, but completely unnecessary to the story my readers want to hear.

I remember arguing with my writing group about a particular passage. I kept insisting that I wanted to include a precious story about something Tolkien did while developing his characters. I loved that story then. I love that story still. But it was long, complicated, and hard to explain, so it clogged up the narrative. It was a speed bump on the way to the point I was actually trying to make. I clung to it anyway.

"I'm keeping it," I said.

Then Dani stepped in. "Stop! Leave it. Airport Man does… not… care."

Airport Man does not care. This became our team's shorthand for "I know *you* love it. But it's *not important* to your intended reader. Leave it out." *Bandersnatch* thrived. That book is what it is because of Dani. And Airport Man.

Picturing an ideal reader offers enormous practical help. When I had to record my classroom lectures during the COVID-19 pandemic, I taped pictures of my students right beneath the camera lens and spoke directly to them. When I was working on *Clay in the Potter's Hands*, I pinned a photo of my friend Linda on the bulletin board above my desktop computer. When I looked at her face, I could feel my shoulders relax, my heart warm. I smiled as I wrote, and the warmth and care I felt for that dear friend made its way into my prose. I can feel it, and now my readers can too.

A reader archetype helps the writer who tries to write "for everyone." That little photo tacked to the wall can help anchor you to your ideal reader, the one who will get the most out of the book because they relate to the specifics it contains.

So try this magic trick: Come up with your own Airport Man. Write out a description or picture a specific person in your life. Who are you trying to reach? Who are you writing for?

Discover the Missing Map

When I told my friend Oscar I was working on a book about writing, he dropped his head and stared at his shoes. "I've always wanted to write a book," he said.

"Really? That's so cool. Do you know what you want to write about?"

He looked up and paused. "Um, yeah. My grandmother."

We talked for a while. As it turned out, his grandmother had been quite a character. Raised in Berlin, she faced terrifying circumstances during the war. It was a miracle that she survived; it was astonishing what she had gone on to accomplish.

But every time he sat down to write about her, he got stuck. Overwhelmed. There were too many possibilities, and all of them were promising. He wanted to describe his grandmother's philosophy of life. He wanted to produce a time capsule, a snapshot of a specific period in history. He wanted to include material about her faith journey and how it sustained her through every difficulty. And there were funny stories he wanted to tell, many of them caused by language barriers as she first adjusted to life in the United States. There were financial troubles, too, and real hardships. She had a huge impact on his life, and he felt inadequate to tell her story. He wanted to do something to honor her memory.

We worked together for quite a while. He already had a purpose. He wanted to honor his grandmother and tell her story. And he had a topic, too. But what was his message? We kept talking, and here is what we came up with: *My grandmother, Oma Wilma, was incredibly resourceful, overcoming almost impossible odds. Not only did she survive, but she also learned to thrive and raise a wonderful family.*

What a great message! Overcoming. Conquering. Prevailing. Surviving. These key concepts helped him to decide what to include and what to leave out. Which events form the backbone of his story, and which details are just background and miscellany? His tone would be one of pride for her accomplishments. And perhaps, taken together, her story would serve a larger purpose—a source of encouragement to others.

We found the center of gravity; we had a purpose, a topic, and a message. So we moved on to the next question: What form should it take? Oscar looked puzzled. I explained that the same story could be told in several different forms or genres:

- A chronological biography, recounting the events of her life story.
- A novel, using the events of her life but in fictional form, based on a true story.
- A collection of essays, each one focused on a different event.
- A first-person narrative, as if Oma Wilma is telling the story of her life in her own voice.
- A scrapbook, including excerpts of her letters and photographs, along with short descriptive essays.
- A collection of essays, each one presenting a different memory.

Oscar didn't think he could manage to write a whole book, whether biographical or fictional. But a collection of essays? That felt manageable if he took them one at a time. He would write ten or twelve essays, each one telling how his grandma overcame one specific challenge, each one representing a different season of Oma Wilma's life.

Perfect!

But I had one more question. "Who is your *audience*?"

It took him a long time to answer. When he spoke, it was almost a whisper. "I am afraid that if I don't write this down, I will forget what happened. And then my daughter will never know what a wonderful role model her great-grandmother was." He had his audience.

What happened in that lunchtime conversation felt like a miracle. Oscar had been weighed down for years. Now he had clarity. Realizing what was at stake changed his determination to tackle the project and see it through. Knowing his purpose, his message, his genre, and his audience gave him the traction he needed to get started. It completely transformed his mood, from dread and confusion to new energy and confidence.

He was smiling when I saw him a few weeks later. He had already picked a specific event in Oma Wilma's life and started to write about it. He was on his way.

Like Oscar, clarifying your purpose, message, genre, and audience can get you moving forward. Talking through these four questions with a friend can be a great way to gain clarity and momentum. Or write them out on a piece of paper and keep them at hand. One sheet of paper can become the first page of your missing map, one that guides you along the pathway to the finish line. A little bit of forethought can make all the difference in the world.

Chapter 3 Summary
ANALYZE

- Every writing project, whether fiction or nonfiction, poetry or prose, is defined by four key factors: our *purpose*, our *genre*, our *message*, and our *audience*.
- Your purpose creates the basis for all future decisions about the work.
- Your genre informs what expectations your reader will bring to your writing.
- Your message tells the reader what you will claim, argue, describe, or explain about your topic.
- You naturally shift your vocabulary, syntax, tone, content, and approach to fit your intended audience, but each variation will remain authentic to who you really are.

The Big Idea

The more clarity we have about the nature of our task, the more likely it is that our path will be easy and our success assured.

Take a Step

Think about various writing projects you have tackled in the past—quick and informal, long and complex, personal or business, private and public. Do you see evidence of the ways your writing changes to adapt to each situation?

Final Word

If we try to present a general topic to a generic reader, it is virtually impossible to write well. We gain traction and writing becomes much easier as we learn all we can about the task at hand: our purpose, our genre, our message, and our audience.

Chapter 4
GATHER
Stockpile Ideas

Have you ever wanted to write but couldn't find the words? Have you ever started with an idea but you quickly ran out of things to say about it? When we fail to understand where ideas come from and neglect to gather them in abundance, we're bound to get stuck. Abigail emphasizes, "Stockpiling ideas is preventative care for writer's block." If we haven't gathered stories, facts, and varied perspectives, we'll run out of ideas quickly. It's like filling the gas tank before embarking on that road trip, putting money into the bank before you try to make a withdrawal, or stocking the refrigerator before you start to make dinner. It is perilous to shortchange this step of the writing process.

In this chapter, we will explore how to stockpile ideas, not only so that you have plenty of material but also so that your content is insightful, substantial, and meaningful. There are many ways for writers to stockpile ideas, whether you feel inspired or not. Mercedes Lackey observes that sometimes our best ideas come from "looking at even the most mundane of things or events and asking yourself the question, 'What if?'" I like that a lot—daydreaming, speculating, and wondering are such important parts of the gathering process.

I also like the way that Christine Hyung-Oak Lee explains it. I appreciate her emphasis on simply being ready. She writes:

> So much of [the creative process] is about waiting. It is about showing up on the steps each day to greet the Muse, should she choose to stop by. You sweep the steps, waiting. Sometimes the Muse does not come by. Oftentimes, the Muse makes no appearance. But if you are not on the steps, and the Muse DOES come by, then you miss her. So you wait.

Lee's imagery is similar to that of Flannery O'Connor, who says, "Every morning between 9 and 12, I go to my room and sit before a piece of paper. Many times, I just sit for three hours with no ideas coming to me. But I know one thing. If an idea does come between 9 and 12, I am there ready for it."

Put it together, and you get something like this:

- You train yourself to pay attention.
- You play with possibilities, maybe putting two different ideas together to see what you get, or asking "What if?"
- You develop the habit of sitting yourself down and getting to work, whether you feel like it or not.
- When good ideas show up, you welcome them, honor them, and find a way to write them down.

I like that emphasis on cultivating a mindset that sets the stage for inspiration. But I confess that I am even more enamored by the brutal advice Jack London has to offer. Where do ideas come from? How do you stay inspired? London's answer is no-nonsense: "You can't wait for inspiration. You have to go after it with a club."

Go after it? With a club?? Yes, really. I'm quite serious. If you want to start strong and maintain your momentum, there are times when you need to get just a little bit aggressive. Don't just show up, pay attention, and take notes, although that's a start.

Go after those ideas. The rest of this chapter will explain how.

Ideas from Within You

The first place to discover good ideas is not out there somewhere. It's you: your own fascinations, opinions, metaphors, and memories. It's the thoughts that flow in and out of your stream of consciousness on any given day. Yet most of these fade quickly, forgotten and undocumented. These ideas are of no use to you unless you grab hold of them. Your job is to pause and pay attention.

Joseph Bentz's writing process is a great example. Joe is an award-winning author and professor of literature. Nothing fascinates me more than listening to him describe the way he begins a novel. Here is what he told me:

> It starts with an image: I can see two people having a conversation, or a man walking along the beach, or a family in a car on a long road trip. If I had to describe it, I would say it is sort of like having a memory of something that never happened. When an image arrives, I pause. I lean into the scene, and I can almost hear their conversation. I grab a scrap of paper or click the note-taking function on my phone, and try to get down as much of the scene as I can. I write down these scenes or bits of dialogue or visuals, and I collect them in a file folder. I have no idea whether I will end up needing them or using them. I may set them aside, or they may become the key to the whole book.

His process is organic and intuitive. It is also anything but passive. Joe hunts down ideas—pausing, listening, paying attention. As a novelist, he is always on the lookout. He welcomes the ideas that show up, then writes them down and stashes them away. He describes gathering as the "Play Stage" of writing a novel. I like that.

Another great writer, Joan Didion, uses a different metaphor to describe this process. Her ideas often start with "pictures that shimmer" in her mind. She pays attention, then goes to work: "I write entirely to find out what I'm thinking, what I'm looking at, what I see and what it means."

If you are writing fiction, be on the lookout for the following:

- A scene slowly coming into focus
- An idea for a character
- A setting you've always wanted to write about
- Something you overheard at the grocery store that would make a great line of dialogue
- A general feeling, mood, or atmosphere you want to create

You may also draw ideas from areas of experience or expertise. John Grisham famously draws inspiration from his career as a lawyer. Many science fiction writers use backgrounds in physics, engineering, or math to build fantastic yet plausible worlds.

If you are writing nonfiction, the gathering process is the same. John McPhee, a prolific and well-respected writer, says, "Ideas are everywhere. They just go by in a ceaseless stream." Our thoughts, our concerns, our fears, our prayers. Things that turn up again and again in conversation; things that preoccupy us when we are supposed to be doing something else; things we keep bringing up every time we talk to our friends.

Reflect on your interests, practice paying attention, and faithfully record what comes to mind:

- Personal experiences
- Stories you've heard from others

- Reflections, assumptions, opinions, frustrations
- A fascinating or troubling statistic
- Takeaways from books, podcasts, social media, or studies
- A perspective that is missing from the conversation
- A problem you want to help others solve

Writing well means permitting yourself to follow your creative genius. A hunch, a question, a puzzle, a clue that might catch your interest can turn into something wonderful and unexpected if pursued. In fact, the impact of your writing starts with changes in you, something that enhances your sense of awe or awakens your curiosity. If you're not intrigued by a topic, how can you expect to engage your readers? It's time to follow that line of questions, unpack that thorny problem, and capture that scene. Make space to daydream, to make new connections, and discover new insights. Then go after them.

Successful writers prime their pen by continually gathering new material and socking it away. Anne Lamott puts it this way: "If you are a writer, or want to be a writer, this is how you spend your days—listening, observing, storing things away."

What interests you? What do you see as an urgent social issue, or a skill that people need to cultivate? What theory, event, or concept seems to lack the right treatment or hasn't yet been adapted for the right audience? What forgotten ideas need to be revisited? What do you long to emphasize, explain, or make clear?

The most important thing, no matter what you are writing, is that you pay attention to what you already know. Stephen King describes the habit of attention this way: "Good story ideas seem to come quite literally from nowhere, sailing at you right out of the empty sky; two previously unrelated ideas come together and make something new under the sun. Your job isn't to find these ideas but to recognize them when they show up."

King is right. We learn to recognize these ideas and then take them a step further and *write them down*. If we don't record them, we'll lose them. The writers in my life find many practical ways to be ready when an idea shows up. Mike carries a tiny spiral notebook in his shirt pocket. Elizabeth frequently uses her phone's voice memo function. Lin has stacks of sticky notes around her house. Brad keeps a folder full of subfolders on the desktop of his laptop. Abigail has a notepad on her phone. And me? I keep a Moleskine journal in my purse and piles of yellow legal pads stashed strategically throughout my house. When an idea, an inspiration, a telling phrase, or an evocative image occurs to me, I am ready for it.

Ideas from Around You

You have an idea. You notice it and write it down. What's next? After documenting the ideas from within you, it's time to start gathering material from other sources. In other words, it's time for research.

To research is to recognize that you are not the first person to address this topic. This doesn't mean your voice isn't needed. It simply means now is the time to discover what else is out there and allow that to shape what you want to say when you finally sit down at the table to speak.

Search the Internet

Most of my students start the gathering process by going online. Internet searches are certainly helpful. But beware: The internet can be a writer's most faithful procrastination tool. Learn to tell the difference between fruitful inquiry and fruitless wanderings. If you start seeing silly cat videos, you've probably gone too far. My friend Teresa reminds me that there is a fine line between research and procrastination. "It's just too easy to get lost in the sauce and never get around to actually writing."

Another concern: The internet is crowded with misinformation, disinformation, shallow assumptions, unsupported claims, trite expressions, and biased notions. It takes a great deal of vigilance to evaluate the information and the opinions you find there. Not only that, it can be tricky to accurately cite all your quotations, summaries, and paraphrases. More and more, research is not so much the art of finding things; it is the art of evaluating and carefully selecting relevant, reliable, compelling data.

Any online search is likely to include something from Wikipedia, which has become "the most popular reference website on the internet." Online encyclopedias are not a bad place to start if you want to accomplish three things: 1) Get a reasonable overview of the scope and substance of a topic, 2) Discover who is considered an expert in the field, and 3) Find up-to-date bibliographies. But keep in mind: The thing that makes a source like Wikipedia so appealing is how easy it is to use. For that reason, some of your readers are likely to view Wikipedia citations as evidence of shallow research.

Whether you are trying to get details right for your novel or writing an opinion piece for a newsletter, you would be wise to expand your search beyond a simple search engine. Consider using curated sites. One important source is Google Scholar, which is designed to provide research-based resources and references. The Library of Congress not only contains written texts, but also photographs, music, art, and more. Google Books contains the full text of many published works, and those texts are searchable. The Digital Commons Network helps writers discover peer-reviewed articles, dissertations, book chapters, and conference proceedings. There are many others, including JSTOR, Scopus, and ResearchGate, with new sites and services constantly being developed. Don't neglect them.

In short, if you stay alert to the limits and dangers, the internet is terrific. But other research strategies may help writers even more.

Read Widely

As I've mentioned, if you want to be a good writer, you have to read. In his memoir, Stephen King writes:

> It's hard for me to believe that people who read very little (or not at all in some cases) should presume to write and expect people to like what they have written, but I know it's true.... Can I be blunt on this subject? If you don't have the time to read, you don't have the time (or the tools) to write. Simple as that. Reading is the creative center of a writer's life.

This idea—becoming well-acquainted with what others have done—is true of all creative work. One of my favorite authors, Mihaly Csikszentmihalyi, puts it this way:

> Artists agree that a painter cannot make a creative contribution without looking, and looking, and looking at previous art, and without knowing what other artists and critics consider good and bad art. Writers say that you have to read, read, and read some more, and know what the critics' criteria for good writing are, before you can write creatively yourself.

There it is again: "read, read, and read some more." While the internet is an expansive universe of information that is super easy to access, reading print resources offers several important advantages. Before a conventional publisher publishes an article or book, it is evaluated by a team of editors.

Don't get me wrong: This does not guarantee accuracy or worth. However, it does represent a process of discernment and selection. Someone else has already made the first cut, as it were, and determined that this work has value.

Read books about your topic and related topics. Read the bestsellers as well as niche voices. This will teach you genre: the different ways to approach your topic or your story. You'll learn style: expanding your vocabulary and learning the music of the sentence. You can survey content: not only to gather data but also to explore what others have already said about the topic and identify what you have to add to the conversation. To paraphrase Walt Whitman, you will discover that "the powerful play goes on." When you write, you are entering into a conversation that has been going on for a long time. When you research, you are primed to contribute your verse.

I Love a Library

If the book is in print, it has received some level of validation. If the book is part of a library collection, it has been judged worthy again, a further step of selection and another indication that the content has been deemed reliable or important.

When it's time to search for books, my college students are quick to access the online library catalog, but the key problem is that a search is only as good as the search terms you use. Pick the wrong term, and your results will be off target. Ignore the right term, and you will never find the most important resources you need. There is a ton of information out there, but it can be hard to find unless you know exactly what to ask for.

So ask a librarian. Librarians have one essential superpower—they know how to find things. And most of them love serving as companions and guides. Author Matt Haig says it best: "Librarians are just like search engines, except they smile and they talk to me and they don't give me paid-for advertising when they are trying to help. And they have actual hearts."

Head for the library. Any library. Your university library, the public library, or even your local community college library. Explain to a library staff member that you need help researching for your project—they can connect you to the right person. Once you're connected, explain your project and your research goals. Librarians are there to help you at any stage, so whether you have absolutely nothing written or are deep into revising your first draft, they can guide your research.

They can help you find books, but give them a chance to shine. They can also locate scholarly journals. They can show you how to navigate databases like ProQuest, EBSCOHost., JSTOR, and Journals and databases offer substantial information produced by experts, rigorously checked and double-checked for accuracy and value.

> Librarians have one essential super-power—they know how to find things.

Note that you don't need to be writing something academic to find great resources in the library. Remember, libraries have all types of books, all available for free.

Here's the only caveat: You need to allow enough time for gathering materials at the library. Procrastinators, take note. Even if you are not planning to start that project anytime soon, taking a trip to your local library to get familiar with it will save you loads of time and frustration down the line. Even just meeting with a librarian to clarify your research question and brainstorm possibilities is a great place to start.

Ideas from Others

You can gather great ideas by reflecting. You can listen to the ongoing conversation by reading and researching. But sometimes, you need a tangible experience—something you can hear, touch, and interact with—to give you ideas and insights, words and phrases, illustrations and examples that you have not yet accessed.

You can think of this source as field work. Some of the richest images and most compelling insights come through this method. And this might be the most fun form of stockpiling yet.

Go on a Field Trip

My students groan—loudly—when I mention the idea of doing research. I get it. I know many writers whose school experience looked like this: They would get an assignment, write their research paper, and then trudge to the library or pillage the internet to search for a handful of relevant quotations to back up what they had to say.

I remember working with one undergraduate who was writing a research paper about sailboats. I saw him in the library one day, poring over photographs of various kinds of boats and taking detailed notes about their various features. When I saw him later, I told him I was glad to see he was making such good progress on his topic.

Then I suggested he do some field research over the weekend. He looked confused, so I asked him, "Why don't you spend a little time at the shore? Talk to some boat owners. Find out what features matter to an experienced sailor."

Spend the weekend in the library or take a trip down to the lake? He chose to spend the weekend by the water, and that not only improved his paper, but it also changed his feelings about the whole writing process.

With many topics, you can get straight to the heart of it by taking a field trip. My friend Dave writes novels and screenplays that include characters from our legal system. Recently, he wrote to tell me how thrilled he was to receive a jury summons. "Wow! A chance to participate firsthand in the messy process of judging a case," he said. Dave understands the value of personal experience to bring his subject to life. The stories he writes are infused with the vibrant details of his firsthand experience.

Another example of this approach is Pixar's movie-making team. Research and development can take up to a year, and field research is an integral part of it. When the Pixar team created *Ratatouille*, they took a trip to Paris to study what it's really like in a French kitchen. For *Coco*, the Pixar team traveled all over Mexico, studying the music, the food, and the customs. Think about how well the colors and textures of that film reflect the heart of that story and its culture. For *Up*, the team traveled to Venezuela to gather inspiration for the fictional landmark of Paradise Falls. The creative team "ventured to the top of the tepuis [flat-topped mountains], took thousands of photos, drew pictures of the landscape and ecosystem, and even laid on their stomachs to peer over the edge to get a true sense of the height and scope for their climactic scenes."

And speaking of details, the Pixar team also traveled along Route 66 to collect dirt samples so they could match the exact colors of the real landscapes they designed for the movie *Cars*.

Much of Pixar's creative vision is the result of firsthand research—and it's fun research, at that. Here is Pixar's secret: "It might seem counter-intuitive, but the best way to get an audience to believe in an imaginary world is by faithfully studying our real one." Doing so adds color, sound, and gritty detail to the story.

Field trips do not require thousands of dollars or a ton of international travel. There are opportunities all around you. If you're writing a fictional scene that takes place on a subway, can you catch a ride and record some details to enrich your description? If one of your characters is a second-language learner, can you sit in on an ESL class? If you're writing about how Gen Z expresses their spirituality, can you visit a Bible study or meet with a youth group? If you're writing about how strangers build connections with one another, can you camp out at a coffee shop and observe the people around you?

How might plunging into life's experiences take your writing out of the virtual and into the solid, the real, and the relatable?

Conduct an Interview

Another engaging, hands-on way to research is by interviewing. What makes the interview such a powerful source of information? For me, no matter how ordinary or tiresome an idea might be, I am always energized when I have the chance to talk with someone who is passionate about the subject.

True story: One of the very best student essays I have ever read was on the topic of crop rotation. Seriously. It's because the student had firsthand experience of living and working on a farm. He knew exactly what's at stake when farmers are careless as stewards of their land. He was deeply invested in the topic, and, as I listened to him tell the story, so was I.

Find people with real-world experience with your topic. While others can give opinions, they can give you a boots-on-the-ground perspective anchored in real life. They can tell you whether the most popular narratives align with reality or miss the mark.

Interviewing is effective because it is vibrant and also because it is current. When you talk with an expert, you can discover the latest developments. You can ask for advice about the most recent resources. You can hear firsthand what terminology, examples, ideas, and research are new and groundbreaking, and which ones are out of date.

In addition, interviews are focused. Sometimes, the information we need is very specific. We don't need the entire context, the extensive nuance, or the practical application. We need to zero in on just one thing. Asking an expert is often quicker than an internet search or hours spent scanning the pages of a journal article or a book, looking for the elusive detail we need.

Interviewing also offers clarity. When you are talking with experts, you can ask them to define terms, give examples, and connect new material to things you already know. As you talk, you can intervene and ask questions if you don't understand something, if the conversation is going too fast, if you are unclear about terminology, or if you don't see why some particular fact is significant. An interview is interactive—you can control the speed and the direction. It's personal. It's human.

Over the years, I've interviewed scholars, teachers, authors, artists, actors, musicians, and others. Some have been little more than a quick question or two after a lecture; at other times, it's longer sessions over coffee or correspondence by letter or email. These personal connections have been delightful and so fruitful.

Who should you interview?

Start small. Often, the most well-known voices on a subject are out of reach. However, many others are eager to share their insights if we're willing to dig a little deeper. Rather than reaching out to a major movie star, best-selling novelist, or world-class scientist, reach out to a blogger you admire, a teacher who offers a class about your topic, the organizer of the online fan club, or someone you heard interviewed on a podcast.

Search Amazon and see what books come up—who are the most popular authors writing on your topic? If you search YouTube, who are the people who have posted lectures about it? Do you know a teacher from high school or college who is connected to your topic? Are there any forums or channels for this topic on LinkedIn, Reddit, Goodreads, Instagram, TikTok, or other social media platforms? Who are the people whose names keep popping up in those spaces?

If you are writing a memoir or autobiography, the interview is one of your most valuable prewriting tasks. Who else remembers the incident you are writing about? What details come to mind for them? What was the significance of the event from their point of view? Find people who were involved. Their insights will enhance your own. Having a multitude of perspectives is priceless.

How do you contact them?

Once you have identified someone you would like to interview, see if they have a website. If so, does it have an email address, contact form, or link to their social media? Send them a message, thank them for their work, then ask one short, simple question. If they respond, you are off to a good start. Build from there.

For one of her essays, Abigail went searching for an expert on parenting. She found that there was a local instructor who offered parenting classes, and her email address was listed on a college's faculty page. The instructor was busy but eager to help someone interested in the important work she does. An ordinary essay turned into something real and urgent, filled with personal stories and key insights.

If an email or contact form is unavailable, there are other ways to reach them. Do you have a mutual connection you can leverage? Are there common events in this community—such as a conference, a book signing, a public lecture, or a webinar—where you could connect and introduce yourself?

Face-to-face interviews are amazing, but don't overlook the possibility of an email, a phone call, or a video interview. If you are hesitating, let me reassure you—people love to know that others are interested in their area of expertise, and it is often easier to get ten or fifteen minutes with an expert than you might think.

MAGIC TRICK

Ask the Right Questions

When I first started working as a journalist, I spent an enormous amount of time preparing lists of questions. I wanted to honor the person and their time, so I would often start with a list of twenty to twenty-five questions, sometimes more. In the interview, I would read through them one at a time, rapid-fire.

As I gained more experience, I realized that my best interviews were the ones that avoided a rigid question-and-answer format. Instead, they had the back-and-forth quality of a good conversation. I made sure to research my subject, and I always started with a short list of key questions that related directly to my subject and my purpose. But the more I did interviews, the more I learned to rely on two important questions. I soon realized that these same two questions formed the bulk of pretty much every interview I ever did. These two questions added the detail, color, and depth I was looking for.

Here's the first question: "Can you tell me more about that?" Most experts have developed a brief "sound bite" answer to a journalist's most common questions. The truth is, many interviewers want nothing more than a short, memorable quotation. But I wanted to go deeper. "Tell me more about that." I wanted to get behind the media persona. I hoped to connect with the person and their passions. I needed to catch a unique insight or a fresh way of thinking that was hiding underneath the slick, rehearsed rote answer. I learned to listen, and then follow up by asking if they could elaborate. Tell me more.

I also wanted something vivid and concrete to add to my story. That's why my other question is, "Can you give me an example?" Nothing brings a situation to life like a real example. It clarifies the meaning, sure, but more importantly, it adds interest and engagement. Collecting information and insight is key. But if you can also collect some great stories, then your writing will come alive.

As it turns out, asking "Can you tell me more about that?" and "Can you give me an example?" have served me well in many other settings. Are they magic? In a way. They have helped me when I am talking with someone in a busy, noisy environment, and I want to find focus. Or I am trying to shift a conversation away from the superficial and make a deeper connection. In many cases, these two questions have paved the way to forging a friendship. Try it.

Rich, Varied, Compelling Content

We've now explored several ways to gather ideas: reflection, reading, field trips, and interviews. Is there such a thing as too many ideas? Not yet. Eventually, you'll need to be selective and narrow your focus. But at this stage, the goal is abundance.

One of my writing teachers, Robert J. Connors, used to say that doing research is like preparing for a New Hampshire winter. Before the snow hits, you take time to gather wood so you can heat your house all season long. You never, ever gather up only the few sticks that you think you will need to get you through December, January, and February. You always gather lots of extra—enough to be certain you will make it through to spring.

And if it turns out you have gathered more than you need? The wood you don't use this month is sure to come in handy later. The ideas you gather now will be the fuel that keeps you writing through the long winter of the drafting stage. Anything you don't use may help your next project. It might make good copy for a blog, newsletter, Instagram post, or short opinion piece. It may serve as the core of a talk you will give, an article you will write, or even the center of your next book. Or it may simply hum along in the background, informing the way you approach your topic, whether or not you specifically include it in the text itself.

As you are gathering ideas for your writing project, take this wise advice from advertising executive Carl Ally:

> The creative person wants to be a know-it-all. He wants to know about all kinds of things—ancient history, nineteenth century mathematics, current manufacturing techniques, hog futures. Because he never knows when these ideas might come together to form a new idea. It may happen six minutes later, or six months, or six years. But he has faith that it will happen.

Maya Angelou underscores the basic principle: "You can't use up creativity. The more you use, the more you have."

The bottom line? Gather more than you need. Assemble a wide range of rich, varied, and compelling content. When you sit down to write, your page will overflow.

Chapter 4 Summary GATHER

- Don't wait around for ideas to find you: Go get them!
- You are your first source for material. Document your stories, memories, impressions, thoughts, and questions—and when ideas show up, welcome them and write them down.
- Be selective when using online sources.
- Read widely to learn what others say and how they say it.
- Get to know local librarians. They are powerful allies in the writing process.
- Have fun with a field trip.
- Tap into the energy and insights of experts through interviews.
- Gather more than you need.

The Big Idea

Gather an abundance of material from a variety of sources.

Take a Step

Consider two or three ways that you can expand your research stage—a field trip, an interview, a visit to the library, or a great book—to make your writing more interesting and your writing process more fun.

A Final Word

Cultivate curiosity and make your writing life a life of discovery.

PART TWO
Maintain Momentum

Don't get it right; get it written.
James Thurber

In PART ONE, the emphasis has been on thinking through your writing process, analyzing your task, and gathering great ideas. These activities will continue as you make your way along the path to come. It can't be said often enough: The writing process is not linear. It involves leaping ahead to proofreading, then looping back to search for fresh ideas; skipping ahead to revise your structure, then circling back to fiddle with your tone and word choice. When football players practice, they focus on perfecting individual skills. But they apply those skills in slightly different combinations every time they are in the game. Of necessity, I am describing these tasks one at a time, but like those players, you will be putting them together into a flexible, recursive process.

In PART TWO, we'll shift our focus from preparation and prewriting to ways of maintaining momentum as you produce page after page of text. It's time to identify your unique workstyle in Chapter 5, then start writing as much as you can as quickly as possible, as described in Chapter 6. This section will also equip you so you know exactly what to do when confronted with your nemesis, whether that is discouragement, perfectionism, worry, distraction, overwhelm, or writer's block, covered in Chapter 7.

Don't stop now. Let's keep going.

Chapter 5
OPTIMIZE
Honor Your Workstyle

Now that we've defined the destination and gathered resources for the journey, it's time to consider how we will get there.

I just met with one of my doctoral students for the first time, a chance for us to get a handle on his dissertation and come up with a specific plan to get it written. As we sat down, Austin launched immediately into describing the books he'd been reading and listing the central ideas he wanted to include. He understood the goal, and he'd done a lot of research and note-taking; in fact, he had gathered a lot of material and was eager to start writing.

"Wait, wait, wait," I told him. "That's great stuff, seriously. We'll talk more about your content in our next meeting, but today our task is to create a plan for writing."

He nodded and proceeded to explain the outline of topics he planned to cover and the two new journal articles he'd just found. I listened and nodded. It was very good—no, it was great.

"I love it!" I said. "You're right. We do need more details about what you have to say. We'll get there. But first, let's talk about how you are going to get your writing done. When will you write? Where will you begin?"

He looked at me blankly.

"Hmm.... I guess I really hadn't thought much about that part."

Perhaps you resonate. Have you ever had an idea or an assignment, figured out what you needed to do, and gathered up dozens of ideas, but had no idea how you'd actually write it? The previous steps are incredibly important, but without a plan for what your writing time will look like, brilliant ideas and loads of research are unlikely to make it onto the page.

As you prepare to draft, you need to get specific about how and when you'll put your seat in the chair. You need to identify your creative rhythms, create a supportive environment, and have a strategy for maintaining momentum when inspiration fades.

"Okay," I said to Austin. "Let's answer some questions about how you write. First, do you like to work from an outline? And do you work better in big, long chunks of time, or do you run out of steam after an hour or two? What do you think? What time of day do your ideas flow the fastest? And when it's time to write, where will you work?"

These questions reveal the essential factors that shape what your writing time will look like. In this chapter, we will explore your options for each one. As we do, reflect on what has worked for you and what has not—what conditions have activated your creativity and which have proven to be obstacles in the path. These observations will shape the way you draft.

Your Preference for Planning

As you move from preparing to drafting, the first question to ask yourself is this: "Do you like to pull your thoughts together by making an outline, or do you prefer to start writing and save organizing for later?"

You have surely encountered teachers or other writers who claim that outlines are an objective requirement to start the writing process. For some, this is super helpful. For others, it's pretty much impossible. Are outlines essential? Your answer depends upon the type of writer you are. Generally speaking, there are two types of writers in this regard: Plotters and Intuitives.

Some writers spend a great deal of time working out the details in their head before they sit down to write a single word. They require an outline or at least a detailed plan before they start writing. Plotters are those who plot out every scene or organize every main point before they can write a word. They love to work it out before they start to write.

But Intuitives can't work that way. They sit down, start writing, and delight to discover their story or message as they go. Intuitives are sometimes called "pantsers," meaning they make progress through their manuscript "by the seat of their pants." They sit down, plunge in, and let the ideas flow, writing page after page of text to figure out what they are trying to say.

What are the technical terms for these two styles? Researchers refer to "Internal Processors," those who are blessed with the ability to plan the overall structure in advance, and "External Processors," those who come to understand their material in the process of actually writing it out.

As we explore each of these two styles, see which one you relate to.

What is a Plotter?

Plotters are writers who need structure to catalyze their creative process. Before they draft anything, they devote significant time to planning and organizing. They may design detailed, multi-layer charts. Sticky notes and color-coding are their friends. They may map out the big picture, listing the main points they want to make in each chapter, or the big scenes, timelines, and character milestones. They devote significant time to this before they write a word.

My friend Tim is a Plotter. When he is working on a novel, he summarizes key scenes on index cards. When he has gathered enough scenes, he spreads the cards across his living room floor, rearranges them, then gathers them up in a deliberate sequence.

Tim writes the whole book by working his way through his stack of cards, scene by scene.

Listen to these Plotters; maybe you can relate.

> "The more time I spend on the outline, the easier the book is to write. And if I cheat on the outline, I get in trouble with the book." –John Grisham

> "Don't start writing without a sturdy table of contents. I probably spent 2 months mulling over this book's table of contents before I began writing the chapters. Nested within the table of contents is an outline for each chapter.... You needn't extensively outline each chapter or even know everything you want to say, but you must have a firm sense of each chapter's purpose and how it contributes to the book's overall purpose." –Paul J. Silvia

> "I'm a plotter. A thinker, a note-maker, a mapper, and a flow-charter. I'm up for using any device that will teach me more about the people I'm writing about and their story."
> –Nick Earls

Working out the details ahead of time helps Plotters avoid problems like plot holes, inconsistencies, awkward proportions, redundancies, and other issues. Plotting allows them to see the big picture of the work and visualize how the components fit together. It frees them to draft with purpose, knowing they have a specific plan that tells them where they are going, even though they may choose to pivot from time to time and adapt along the way.

There are a great many famous Plotters. James Patterson is one of the best-selling English-language authors of all time, with more than 400 million copies sold. He is a complete Plotter. Joseph Heller's *Catch 22* is "the product of acute compositional rigor—with all the pieces, scenes, characters, and events interlinking and joined together in a clear narrative." William Faulkner wrote the complete chapter outline for *A Fable* on the walls of his bedroom. Henry Miller, Norman Mailer, Tim Powers, and Sylvia Plath are other celebrated writers who start with meticulous plans.

What is an Intuitive?

On the other hand, Intuitives plunge right in and start drafting. They sit down and write, and the writing itself is what primes the pump. It's like they are listening for the words and phrases to come to them, and then they sit and write them down. As they write, they are often surprised by the tone, length, direction, characters, conflicts, and even the events that show up on the page. Start with an outline? No way. That doesn't work for an Intuitive. To paraphrase Graham Wallas, they don't know what they think until they see what they say.

Listen to these Intuitives; maybe you can relate:

> "I like to think of the book as being an adventure. I have this mantra which says, Serve the story, listen to the story. And often the story knows better than I do what it wants to be." –David Morrell

> "The big benefit I have found of pantsing a novel is that it allows you as a writer to get creative, to take risks, to try new things. Each day when you sit down to write, you decide in that moment what direction the story will take, which could be completely different from what you wrote yesterday, or what you will write tomorrow." –Sassafras Lowrey

> "It's just like you can't plot tomorrow or next year or ten years from now. When you plot books, you take all the energy and vitality out. There's no blood. You have to live it from day to day and let your characters do things." –Ray Bradbury

"I do whatever the beat feels like, whatever the beat is telling me to do. Usually, when the beat comes on, I think of a hook or the subject I want to rap about almost instantly. Within four, eight bars of it playing, I'm just like, 'Oh, OK. This is what I wanna do.'" –Eminem

Morrell, Lowrey, Bradbury, and Eminem are Intuitives. Another famous Intuitive is J. R. R. Tolkien. Tolkien spent an enormous amount of time devoted to prewriting: He made paintings, invented languages, and drew maps and intricate genealogies. But when it came to drafting the story itself, he plunged in and let it unfold as he wrote. "I have long ceased to invent," he said. "I wait till I seem to know what really happened. Or till it writes itself."

In describing his work on *The Lord of the Rings*, Tolkien observes:

> I met a lot of things on the way that astonished me. Tom Bombadil I knew already; but I had never been to Bree. Strider sitting in the corner at the inn was a shock, and I had no more idea who he was than had Frodo. The Mines of Moria had been a mere name; and of Lothlórien no word had reached my mortal ears till I came there. Far away I knew there were the Horse-lords on the confines of an ancient Kingdom of Men, but Fangorn Forest was an unforeseen adventure. I had never heard of the House of Eorl nor of the Stewards of Gondor. Most disquieting of all, Saruman had never been revealed to me, and I was as mystified as Frodo at Gandalf's failure to appear on September 22.

Tolkien wasn't surprised by his story: He was *astonished* by it. Key characters and essential places came into focus after he sat down at his desk and started writing. Not only that, Tolkien wrote *The Lord of the Rings* without anticipating key aspects of the plot.

Donald M. Murray was also an Intuitive. He was working on a novel when I took a class with him in the summer of 1986. One day, we asked him how he was coming along with a pivotal chapter he had been working on. His answer: "I've just gotten the son to the hospital where my main character will finally confront his old man. I can't wait to get home and start writing so I can find out what he is going to say." Murray did not design his stories. He made it a habit to schedule writing time. Then he showed up, and the story revealed itself as he wrote.

Are You a Plotter, an Intuitive, or a Bit of Both?

As you look toward drafting, should you outline first? Well, that depends. Are you more comfortable with a plan in hand, or would you rather improvise? Do you resonate more with the Plotter or the Intuitive?

If you are a Plotter, then yes. You probably do need to create at least a rough outline before you start writing, especially if you are writing something lengthy like a long essay, a dissertation, a novel, or a whole series. A formal outline is one option, but consider other ways to get organized. Listing, chunking, color coding, or illustrating key plot points may help. Or writing key scenes or concepts on index cards and moving them around to determine the best sequence. Look online to learn about visual outlines, one of my favorite writing tools. Use every available strategy to get a handle on the big picture. Be patient as you prepare.

If you are an Intuitive, then no. You do not need an outline before you start drafting. Follow your creativity, and see where it leads. At some point, you may find that a "reverse outline" is helpful. Rather than creating an outline and then writing from that outline, you reverse those steps. Just write. Then pause from time to time to sketch a rough outline of what you have already written, summarizing the overall structure that has organically emerged. Getting a bird's eye view of your progress allows you to check your organization, revising your sequence and proportion as needed.

As you reflect on your experience as a writer, you may find that while you prefer one style or another, you combine a bit of both the Plotter and the Intuitive. This is true for me as well. In my own process, I typically start with a goal and a rough plan. I'll list or pencil sketch the main sections, creating chunks, and then I'll rough out a possible order for the material. Because I am a visual learner, I often use a large artist's sketchpad for this initial plan. Novelist Brandon Sanderson calls this kind of low-commitment plan a "floating outline." I don't worry about finding the best chunks or the most effective order at this stage. It's too early for me to know how my ideas will ultimately take shape. But I like to have a rough roadmap, just enough structure to get me started. I think of it sort of like a road trip. I have a sense of where to start, I know roughly where I want to end up, and I have identified some of the key stops along the way. And I also know that as I write, I'll make unexpected discoveries, and I need to be open to change, or even, in some cases, a radical new direction.

I also recognize that the amount of planning and preparation I do will vary depending on a number of external factors. For one thing, I use different strategies depending on the genre of the work. While nonfiction starts with a rough plan or "floating outline," creative writing (like a short story, poem, or play) usually starts with a single phrase or line, or perhaps a vivid image. I rarely know where it will go. I noodle around, and the text emerges. It feels more like listening than composing.

You may have discovered that you also use different methods for the different genres you write. I think of my favorite writer, C. S. Lewis. He was an internal processor, meaning that he had the ability to work out the text in detail before he put pen to paper. Once Lewis had completed a mental draft, he wrote it fairly rapidly, sometimes writing an entire book in a matter of weeks. But his poetry? An entirely different process. Lewis wrote draft after draft after draft of his poems, sometimes adjusting the word order, and sometimes adding or deleting entire sections. Here's what's really interesting: Lewis continued to revise his poems even after they were published. He revised some of the same lines for decades, and the sheer number of variations is astonishing. Like C. S. Lewis's, your approach may vary depending on whether you are writing research papers, working on your novel, or assembling a poetry collection.

These different approaches—Plotters, Intuitives, or some combination—are equally valid. However, sometimes it seems that Plotters are praised and Intuitives condemned. I remember many times when a teacher asked me to submit an outline for a research paper several weeks before the paper was due. But here's the problem: I couldn't do that. I couldn't for the life of me write an outline until I had written at least a very rough first draft of the project. I'm too intuitive. So I would go ahead and do all my research, write the whole paper, then outline the paper I had written, and turn that in.

The more experience I have as a writer, the more open I am to experimenting and combining the best of both styles. For me, that means using insights and techniques from each point of view. For you? Lean into your strength. Give your creativity what it needs—be it a roadmap or an open canvas—and experiment with other techniques as needed.

Your Circadian Rhythms

As you think through the patterns and habits that serve you best as a writer, you also want to consider your biorhythms. After all, our physical bodies are integral to our creativity. It's easy to assume that writing is merely an intellectual enterprise—but is it? One of my teachers used to remind the class, "You are not a brain on a stick."

A key aspect of preparing to be a productive writer is thinking through the rhythms of your day. When do you feel most energetic? Most clear-headed? Most optimistic?

When I was in college, I was a night writer. After I finished my classes and had done all my homework, after we'd watched Johnny Carson, after my roommate was fast asleep and the dorm was quiet, I would write. I loved the late-night hours.

Give your creativity what it needs—be it a roadmap or an open canvas.

But my life changed as I got older. These days, my best hours are first thing in the morning, so I write before I leave for work. During summer break, I can usually gather enough momentum in the morning to carry me through to early afternoon, getting in seven or eight hours in a day. But it is virtually impossible for me to be creative if I try to start a writing session in the afternoon or evening. That's why I've learned to guard those morning hours.

Late nights. Afternoons. Early mornings. We need to discover our own best time of day. But what if our options are limited? The truth is, we don't always have control over our schedule, so there are times when we need to let go of the ideal and work with what we can actually manage. The most important thing is not necessarily achieving an ideal but finding a time we can sustain.

Let me tell you about one writer I coached through the first draft of her first book. I'll call her The Lunchtime Novelist. She worked full-time and had four kids at home. In the morning, it was all she could do to get the kids up and on their way to school, then rush out the door to clock in at the office. Coming home at the end of the day was the same—coordinating rides, making dinner, cleaning up, supervising homework, and finagling bedtimes. By the time the last little one was asleep, she could not have managed a single coherent sentence. She went to bed.

So how did she manage to write that novel? She asked her boss if she could arrive at work thirty minutes early and then take ninety minutes for her lunch break instead of an hour. She found a quiet table in a seldom-used conference room. She headed there at lunchtime every workday, ate the sandwich she had packed, and managed a solid hour of writing time five days a week. Her story flourished. And so did she.

Your Natural Cadence

The next big question that helps writers develop and refine their best process is this: What is your writing rhythm? One of the biggest differences that I have found among writers is whether they write best in a steady rhythm, predictable and methodical, or whether they need a big block of time—four or five hours at least, ten or twelve if they can get it—to get their head into the project and make significant progress.

What is a Methodical Writer?

When it comes to writing, I am like an old workhorse. I get up in the morning, grab coffee, and as the caffeine takes hold, I sit down at my writing desk, and I write. After a few hours, I feel like I am just pushing the words around on the page rather than making real progress. That's how I know that I'm done for the day. Usually, it's two or three or sometimes four hours of productive writing every morning, six days a week. After my writing time, I'll get breakfast, do a few household chores, and get ready to head off to school.

I'm methodical. Slow and steady. Boring and predictable. It's a pattern that works for me in this season of my life. Does this sound like you? Are you someone who needs to chip away at a big project day by day, making slow and steady progress? If so, you're a methodical writer. Lean into it. Protect your daily rhythms and keep chugging along.

What is a Binge Writer?

You may be horrified at the thought of my cab-horse approach. Whether it's the demands of your schedule or the steps you go through to cajole the Muse, working on a major project one hour or two each day doesn't work for you. In fact, trying to work this way would drive you right up the wall.

You may be the kind of writer who needs time to cultivate the headspace that makes writing possible. It takes more than an hour or two just to settle your soul and remember what you are doing. It may be three or even four hours before you even *start* to find your focus, pushing past distractions, muddy thinking, and wordless staring. Good for you. You are a binge writer.

Binge writers thrive when they schedule long blocks of time to write. Many find that working a couple of hours on a Friday night, getting organized and warming up, then writing all day on Saturday, head down and pushing through, works well. Binge writers benefit from dedicated vacations and week-long writing retreats.

Whichever pattern has worked best for you, you might try experimenting with a bit of each style. I am not a binge writer, but sometimes I need to give my project my full attention. When I am faced with a tricky problem or a complex research challenge, I give myself more time. When I have finished a draft of a longer work—a whole book, a complicated series of lectures—I try to get away for a day or two so I can stop staring at individual sections and read the entire work as one integrated whole. Conversely, if you're naturally a binge writer, you may need to plod along for a while in smaller blocks of time until your schedule opens up and you're able to plan a few of those longer stretches.

Methodical writer? Binge writer?

One of the secrets to becoming a better writer and finally getting that project done is being honest about your creative rhythms and then scheduling sessions that work for you. What pattern is realistic, given the realities of your life and the needs you have as a creative? A little bit each day? Three blocks of time each week? A full day and a half every other week, where you clear the decks and do nothing else other than write, write, write, write, write? Think about it, then create your plan.

Your Most Productive Environment

So far, we've covered your preference for planning and the creative rhythms that feel most natural. Let's talk about one more essential piece of your practical writing plan: Where will you write? By that I mean both the physical place and the specific environment you create.

Many people think that the best way to be productive is to grit their teeth and try harder. But Studies of highly innovative people suggest that you can dramatically increase your productivity and originality by adjusting your workspace. Mihalyi Csikszentmihalyi is emphatic. "It is easier to enhance creativity by changing conditions in the environment than by trying to make people think more creatively."

When I am working with my student writers, I'll ask them to consider the environmental conditions that support their best writing. I put them into small groups, and I have them discuss the following factors. You certainly don't have to decide all these before you begin, but pay attention to which ones resonate with your times of flow state and which you might like to try.

Location: Home? Library? Starbucks? Denny's? A sunny patio? A bench in the park? An empty classroom?

Space: Open windows or private and enclosed? Cluttered or clean? Cozy or spacious?

Seating: At a desk? At a big dining room table? On the couch? Leaning up against a pile of pillows in bed? Curled up in a favorite chair? Sprawled on the floor?

Lighting: Natural lighting to boost your mood? Dim lighting to promote feelings of safety, encouraging vulnerability and honesty? Bright, clear light to signal focus?

Temperature: Cool and refreshing? Warm and inviting?

Inspiration: Favorite photos, a stuffed animal, fresh flowers? Or perhaps a meaningful, inspiring object like a childhood toy, a rock, a favorite quotation, or a religious symbol?

Sound: Music? Netflix? Friends? Utter silence? The ambient buzz of a coffee shop or café? An app or website that produces nature sounds, such as rain or ocean waves, or a musical soundtrack?

Timekeeping: A watch, clock, or timer?

Beverages: Red Bull? Hot cocoa? Coffee? Diet Dr. Pepper? Tea, Earl Grey, hot?

Snacks: M&M's? Red licorice? Skittles? Snickers? Salty chips? Pretzels?

What are the conditions that comfort, inspire, and sustain you as you write? Attention to small details, like sitting by a big window, listening to a particular kind of music, or having your preferred snack on hand, can make a big, big difference.

Engaging your senses can help you achieve a flow state. Listening to music is one example. Is there a particular style of music that helps you focus as you write? Have you designed a playlist that supports your work? Today, I am listening to folk guitar music in the background—Phil Keaggy mostly, with a touch of Trace Bundy and Andy McKee. Other times, I tune in to the local classical music station. I vary my music depending on what I need and where I am in the writing process. Do I need a gentle mood to help me as I wrestle with a tricky passage? Something to enliven and energize me as I am gathering fresh ideas? Or absolute silence as I face the blank page and search for the right words?

Research has also shown that your sense of smell can help to enhance your concentration. Lighting a candle can calm your mind and reduce stress as you settle in. It can also simply serve as a ritual that signals to your brain you are about to sit down and work for a while. As Anne Lamott reminds us, "Rituals are a good signal to your unconscious that it is time to kick in."

Do you have snacks on hand? From time to time, if the writing isn't going well or if a section is particularly resistant, I crave something salty and crunchy: popcorn, pretzels, or potato chips. I am in good company. Studies show that when people are trying to attack a difficult problem or calm their jitters, they tend to crave salty, crunchy foods. On the other hand, you may be drawn toward the sweet rather than the savory: candy, cookies, or chocolate. Which snacks renew your focus? Which ones bog you down? As you write, are you drinking a Coca-Cola Classic or a decaf coconut milk latte with an extra shot? Sipping from a water bottle or indulging in a bright green energy drink?

As you prepare and then begin to draft, arm yourself with various sounds, scents, and flavors. Pay attention to the effect they have. As you go, you'll decide if some supplies are most helpful at certain times of day, certain stages of the writing process, or with particular kinds of writing. Experiment and discover what works best for you.

MAGIC TRICK
A Four-Hour Block of Time

Whether you are a Plotter or an Intuitive, a night writer or an early bird, a binge writer or a methodical one, you should be aware of some important research that's been done on the science of creativity.

Cal Newport has coined the phrase "deep work" to describe the kind of focus and flow that creative breakthroughs demand. He describes the principle this way: "Deep work is the ability to focus without distraction on a cognitively demanding task." And that certainly includes writing.

While this type of "deep work" or "flow state" can be difficult to activate, numerous studies across different disciplines suggest that there is something magical about a four-hour block of time. Think about it. How long can you maintain peak focus and stay on task? For most of us, the answer is about four hours. It seems that a shorter block of time does not allow us to settle down, shut out distractions, and completely focus on the task. On the other hand, more than four hours without a break can lead to fatigue, fuzzy thinking, and lowered energy. Musicians, computer programmers, chess players, and others who engage in intense, deliberate practice find that after about four hours of focused time, their performance begins to decline.

In *The Paris Review* interviews, journalists conducted more than four hundred in-depth interviews with professional, accomplished writers. In those interviews, and in other conversations with effective writers, the idea of a four-hour block of time comes up again and again.

> Aldous Huxley: "I usually work four or five hours a day. I keep at it as long as I can, until I feel myself going stale."

Stephen King: "I write about 2,000 words a day, five days a week. It takes me about four hours."

F. Scott Fitzgerald: "I would work about three to four hours a day, and I would set a goal of 1,000 words. I wanted to write something every day, even though it wasn't always easy."

Alice Munro: "I write every morning, seven days a week, starting about eight o'clock and finishing around eleven."

Anthony Trollope: "I wake at 5 a.m. and write through to 8:30 a.m., with a watch on my desk, ensuring 250 words every 15 minutes."

R. L. Stine: "Every day I get up at like 9:30–10, I sit down and I write 2,000 words, and then I quit."

Not so famous? That's okay. A quick search of contemporary authors suggests that this four-hour pattern serves all writers well. Leo Babauta writes, "I have two or three things I really want to write each day, and I write them as early in the day as possible. That's usually 2–4 hours of writing a day (sometimes more)." Mark Douglas Doran says, "Three focused hours, repeated daily, will outproduce ten distracted ones."

The consensus is something like this: My best writing happens in a three- to four-hour session where I aim to complete 1,000 to 1,500 words.

I love the candor in this recent post from Natasha Pulley: "Seeing lots of people beating themselves up for NOT DOING ENOUGH WRITING, so I'd just like to point out that my productive day is about four hours long. Then I collapse. This is because writing is like running. Do not expect to sprint all day."

It's undeniable. The duration of our writing time can affect our focus, which in turn impacts our productivity. I discovered that for myself while working on my dissertation. Long days of writing tended to produce diminishing returns. The more I buckled down, the fewer words I was able to eke out. But an hour here and an hour there didn't work for me either.

Here's what I discovered: There are a lot of aspects of the writing process that I can do in small chunks of time. I can research for fifteen or twenty minutes. I can look up a reference for a footnote, create a scratch outline, straighten up my desk, check my topic sentences, or fiddle with my formatting. I can edit or proofread for ten minutes at a time; in fact, I do a better job of close editing when I work in very short, very focused increments. But when it comes to drafting, about four hours is magic for me. Less than that, and I never get deeply engaged. More than that? I start to fatigue, and my productivity drops like a stone.

Don't force it, but consider giving the four-hour block a try. Experiment, observe, and find out how long you can immerse yourself completely without burning out. Finding your own sweet spot, your most productive time frame: That's magic.

Putting Together Your Plan

How do you pull these insights together to create a system that helps you make steady progress? Let's look at how my doctoral student made his plan. At our first meeting, we reviewed his writing habits and discussed the best way to structure his time, conserve his energy, and keep him focused. We needed to design a pathway he could follow. Completing a doctoral dissertation is no joke.

Plotter or Intuitive? Austin is definitely an Intuitive writer. I told him that Intuitive writers tend to write almost twice as much material as they need, so he should let himself write page after page without editing. Just get it down. Just keep going. I also advised him to pause from time to time, review his pages, and quickly scribble a rough outline in pencil on a scrap of paper. Or if his word processor facilitates it, create headings and subheadings, and step back to see how the work as a whole is shaping up. I suggested creating a scratch outline whenever he felt stuck to help him regroup and restart his creative flow by revealing gaps and offering new insights.

Methodical writer or binge writer? He's bursting with ideas, and so, as you can imagine, it takes him a while to settle down and make progress. He's a binge writer. Once Austin has answered emails, made phone calls, double-checked some favorite online sites, gathered his books and notes, talked to his roommates, grabbed a few snacks, and found his favorite pen, he can finally settle down to write. And once he finds his focus—what Csikszentmihalyi calls *flow*—he can write for four hours, or more, without stopping.

Morning, noon, or night? Early, early morning, as it turns out. He can't manage to sleep past 4:00 a.m. He's up, showered, and checking his email by 4:30 in the morning. Good. I could never function that way, but that's what works for Austin.

We got practical and made a specific plan. He pulled out his calendar, and we built writing time into his schedule: two five-hour blocks each week, starting first thing in the morning every Tuesday and Friday, plus one thirty-six-hour overnight writing retreat every six weeks. (I'll say more about writing retreats in Chapter 12.)

Quiet room or noisy café? Austin decided he preferred the firm chair at his kitchen table to the one in his office. It felt inspiring to be in a room that caught the first rays of morning light. He also decided on a café he could transition to for a change of scenery as needed. After he left my office, he bought some snacks in preparation for the long drafting hours ahead.

Austin added specific work times to his calendar and committed to them. So far, his progress has exceeded his expectations—and mine.

What does your plan look like? What level of structure will help you get going? Given your natural focus times and the realities of your schedule, what time of day is most likely to suit you? Will you make progress in lots of baby steps or a few great leaps? There are no right or wrong answers—what matters is staying true to what you need.

Chapter 5 Summary
OPTIMIZE

- Become aware of what writing habits work for you.
- Plotters benefit from outlining and organizing before they write; Intuitives discover their content and structure as they write.
- Early birds are fresh and creative in the morning; night owls flourish when others are fast asleep.
- Methodical writers make steady progress day by day; binge writers require big blocks of time to find their focus and stay on task.
- Your environment makes a big difference. Variables such as light, sound, seating, and snacks can optimize your environment for creative flow.
- The research of Cal Newport, Csikszentmihalyi, and others underscores what many creatives have discovered: Productivity peaks when we think in terms of a four-hour block of time.

The Big Idea

Our writing process is constrained by our season of life and the nature of our project, but we are more productive when we work with—not against—our personal rhythms.

Take a Step

What are one or two things that you know for sure about your innate workstyle? What are one or two habits you'd like to experiment with?

A Final Word

We don't always have the opportunity to create our ideal circumstances, but if we know what works best for us, we can make better choices about where, when, and how we write.

Chapter 6
DRAFT
Write Fast

Drafting is your first attempt to get your thoughts out of your head and onto the page. You rev up your Word file, Google Doc, yellow pad, pencils, or recording device, and finally begin writing down your content. A first draft is like the pencil sketch that an artist creates on their canvas before they begin to paint: It sets the tone and defines the main contours. Details and refinements come later. As Anne Lamott reminds us, "Almost all good writing begins with terrible first efforts. You need to start somewhere."

The goal here is to just get it *down* in any way you can. I love the way author Shannon Hale describes this stage of the process: "I'm writing a first draft and reminding myself that I'm simply shoveling sand into a box so that later I can build castles." Keep this mindset: You don't have to build the castle just yet. You just have to collect your thoughts all in one place so you are ready to refine them.

Some of the sand will not become part of the sandcastle. Many of the words you write will not make it to the final version. Knowing this, write generously. Put thoughts into words. Put images into descriptions. Put action into scenes. Put lines into poetry.

Writing is a complex, demanding task. Trying to get every aspect of your manuscript right the first time leads to frustration.

That's why the goal for your draft is *not* a finished, polished manuscript. It's just your first crack at it.

As you learn to see writing as a layered, multi-step process, you can give your full attention to one specific issue at a time. After all, there are several steps after this one.

This chapter will help you make your way from blank page to that first rough draft. As Robert Cormier says, "The beautiful part of writing is that you don't have to get it right the first time."

Materials and Tools

The first step when you sit down to draft is to choose your tools. Word processors, pens and pencils, legal pads, and post-its. Are you the type of person who can't resist shopping for office supplies, even though your "back to school" days are long behind you? I would encourage you to invest thoughtfully in materials that sustain you and help you take your work seriously.

What tools help you organize your ideas? I write on a computer, usually using Word or a Google Doc. Many writers swear by drafting in favorite programs like Scrivener or Notion. The processor you choose will, in part, determine how you visualize the big picture of your material. Does it include a feature that lets you see just your outline or major sections? Does it include tools for revising? For sharing your text? If you're working with other writers or plan to get regular feedback, you'll want a program that allows for easy collaboration and multiple users.

On the other hand, analog processing may better suit some projects. When I am writing poetry, for example, I still prefer a sharp pencil and a legal pad. I know many fiction writers who handwrite their stories and then revise and edit as they type them into the computer.

We process electronic information very differently from the tactile experience of the printed page. Sometimes, I feel fatigued, but it's not really because I am tired. It's just that I am tired of looking at a screen. When you lose steam, try handwriting a section of text or printing something out and reading through it, pen in hand, to refresh your perspective and regain your momentum. Leaving the keyboard and working with physical text feels like a completely different task, even if I am working on the exact same project. It refreshes my perspective and keeps me moving forward.

Sometimes, I turn to the note-taking function on my phone. There have been times that I've labored all morning to eke out a few paragraphs and then felt stuck. But an hour later, as I'm driving around and running errands, the perfect wording or best possible example suddenly occurs to me. I either make a quick recording on my phone or, even better, have my phone "send a message to Diana Glyer." When I am back at my desk, there is an email waiting for me with three paragraphs of text. Magic.

Many writers find that the easiest, most natural way to write is to dictate. This is especially true for the verbal processors out there who find the right words more easily through speech or conversation. It's also a life-saving tool for those who are very busy. They can dedicate time while driving or doing other tasks to thinking about their book, speaking their ideas, and downloading a transcription. When they do have time to sit at a computer, they can organize, clarify, and build on those ideas rather than starting from scratch.

Choose your tools wisely. Once you've made your selection, it's time to fill up the page.

MAGIC TRICK

Postpone the Introduction

What is the most important paragraph of your book, essay, or story? The first paragraph. What is the hardest part of your book, essay, or story to write? Yeah, that's right. The first paragraph. Then the first page. Then the first chapter.

It makes sense when you think about it. It's really hard to "introduce" something that doesn't exist yet. Imagine how awkward it can be when you are at a gathering, and you try to introduce someone you hardly know. You can't help being vague, bumbling, and unfocused.

For many writers, the single most powerful piece of writing advice they will ever receive is this: You do not need to start with the introduction. An introduction is a promise that you make to your reader. And when you make that promise, you need to deliver.

When I sit down to begin a new draft, I almost always start exactly the same way. I open a new Word doc, and I write the words "PUT INTRODUCTION HERE." Then I skip down a few lines and start writing whatever part of the project—a key point, a great story, a series of great quotations—feels clearest in my mind. This has a powerful, almost magical effect of removing one of the biggest obstacles to good writing: settling down and getting the first few words down.

Start Anywhere

Save the introduction or opening scene for later. Okay: What next? Many authors are delighted and energized when they realize there is absolutely no reason they must write Chapter 1 before Chapter 2, or before Chapter 20. While we *read* from beginning to end, we do not need to *write* that way. Forcing ourselves to start at the beginning is often counterproductive. After all, we are still discovering. It is freeing to cast off this imaginary constraint.

Start writing with whatever section beckons you. Start with the idea, story, insight, or scene that is clearest in your mind as you sit down to write. Or start with the section of your outline that feels most fully formed, most complete.

"Start anywhere" applies to fiction and nonfiction alike. I am not a novelist, but I have been told that those who write novels can often picture a specific scene in their minds, almost as if they are watching a movie. The protagonist is buying rice at the grocery store when she runs into a college roommate. The couple is sitting at an outdoor café, and the conversation takes an unexpected turn. The child goes out her front door to grab her bike, and it is missing. Storytellers often start by writing that compelling scene first, then building the story out from there.

The temptation, of course, is to say "Yes, but that scene doesn't occur until the midpoint of the story. First, I have to set the scene and introduce the characters and…." That is all true of the finished draft. But it is not true of the writing process. Typically, the words show up as hunches, random phrases, or fleeting images. As they show up, skip around. Write them down.

Just start, and when you run out of steam, move on to the next section and start again. For fiction writers and playwrights, this may be from one scene early in the story to another much, much later. For poets, this may look like jotting down one phrase or a single line and then sitting quietly as you listen for another. For scholarly works such as research articles, start by clustering facts and quotations and grouping them into sections. For short works like a blog post, or nonfiction books that explain or describe, start with one key idea, central claim, illuminating quotation, or simple list. This is the perfect time to listen to the Muse, start where she beckons, and follow where she leads.

Write as Quickly as You Can

If you struggle even a little bit with perfectionism-induced writer's block, the best advice I know is to write your drafts as quickly as you can. This is what Murray calls "outracing the censors," getting through the draft so fast that the voices of negativity and despair don't stand a chance. He observes: "It is important to write the first draft as fast as possible to escape them, not worrying about making sense or following the rules of language, so we can discover what has been hidden in our minds."

Racing through our first draft helps us stay in the flow and avoid the temptation to edit as we write. Tackling too many steps at once is a recipe for overwhelm. If I try to edit as I write, or to assess the work as I am creating it, it's like trying to run a whole 26.2-mile marathon while looking back over my shoulder. Editing and proofreading are important, but it can be your make-or-break moment if you decide to press on rather than look back. Keep the words flowing instead of pausing to second-guess every sentence, phrase, or word choice.

There is an additional benefit of quick writing that is just as important. When you write fast, you take more risks. As a result, your writing will be more dynamic, authentic, and innovative. If you are lucky, you may end up with something far better than anything you could have planned. If you keep a tight rein on every sentence, your writing can begin to feel formulaic and predictable. Write quickly, and stay open to unexpected possibilities.

Write as Badly as You Dare

There are a few principles that are absolutely priceless when it comes to improving your writing, and this is one of them: Lower your standards for your first draft.

Imagine yourself sitting at your writing desk, on your couch, or in a café. Settling in, you write a paragraph. It doesn't sound right. You delete it and start over. You write it again, but it's still not quite right. The word you used to describe the main character in sentence two feels cheesy. You spend fifteen minutes searching for synonyms. You rewrite the paragraph, but it's still not how you envisioned it. You feel embarrassed by the idea of someone reading it. You compare yourself to your favorite author, thinking surely, they'd *never* write a sentence like that. You delete three sentences. You check the time, and it's been an hour. Your writing time is up, and you have one single, polished sentence staring back at you. You have 38,000 words to go to finish your manuscript. You sigh and then spend the rest of the day questioning the life decisions that have led you to try to write this thing in the first place.

Sound familiar? That may or may not have been my exact experience while drafting that particular paragraph.

If you've experienced this, you know how hard it is to stop constantly editing yourself and *get it down*. Writing without editing is a challenge because, as we discussed in Chapter 2, we don't often see other writers' messy first drafts. We assume everyone else's thoughts rush forth in a polished, final form: the published book, the completed article, the prize-winning poem. Or we figure that since we've been at this for a while and have several successful projects under our belt, we should have figured this out by now. Donald M. Murray describes this challenge:

> Many people believe writing comes to the writer like a computer printout, flowing along, finished, complete. Writing usually comes in fragments—details, hints, clues, collisions of information, half ideas, quarter ideas, bits of pieces of information, scraps that have fallen out of books, from TV or radio, from conversations at the next table or in another room. The writer plays with these scraps to see what they may mean.

If we don't believe that everyone's first drafts are messy, the chaos of our first drafts can trigger our imposter syndrome. We're embarrassed to put something down that's not brilliant. We overthink, second-guess, and hit "delete."

And in the meantime, our inner critic chatters away, sounding something like this:

"You can't write."
"Why would anyone care what you have to say?"
"Why are you even doing this anyway?"
"You aren't a very good writer, are you?"

Anne Lamott calls this "The voice of the oppressor." Who could possibly draft anything honest, helpful, true, beautiful, or powerful under the influence of this negative soundtrack? We must do everything we can to overcome this oppressive voice.

By the way, beginning writers often assume that once they become experienced enough, they will no longer deal with the inner critic's nagging voice. Not true. The doubts don't go away with practice. If anything, the pressure only increases. The inner critic keeps at it: "You've been writing for *how many years*, and you still can't get it right?" Then shame. "You published a best-seller? Then why does the paragraph you just wrote sound like a third grader wrote it?" Simply put, the longer we write and the more we publish, the more we expect from ourselves, making it harder for us to relax as we write a first draft without judgment.

Lamott brings the message home, saying, "I know some very great writers, writers you love who write beautifully and have made a great deal of money, and not one of them sits down routinely feeling wildly enthusiastic and confident. Not one of them writes elegant first drafts." Not one of them. Not one.

In trying to avoid the messiness, we end up editing our words to death even before they hit the page. We fall victim to a self-defeating cycle in which we never get our words down on paper, so we can never move forward. As Jodi Picoult gently reminds us, "You can't edit a blank page."

We free ourselves from this tyranny by writing as badly as we dare. Paul J. Silvia expresses it well: "Your first drafts should sound like they were hastily translated from Icelandic by a non-native speaker." Former Pixar president Ed Catmull calls these nascent ideas the "ugly babies" of creativity; they are underdeveloped, but they must be welcomed and nourished, or they'll never have the chance to grow. Anne Lamott puts it succinctly: "The first draft is the down draft—you just get it down. The second draft is the up draft—you fix it up."

The key? Learn to tolerate the awkwardness and the mess just long enough to produce a ragged, rough draft. Do what you can. Just get it down. If you combine low standards with speed, you'll outpace the inner critic. Writing will start to feel less like labor and more like fun.

Tricks to Keep You on Track

As you draft, there will always be speed bumps, potholes, or barriers along the path. Whatever you call them, problems arise, and they threaten to slow (or completely block) your progress. Even small challenges, like looking for a citation or trying to find a good synonym, can threaten to derail you. Bigger ones, like not knowing how to end a chapter, can seem like a major roadblock.

The truth? They're not. You can cruise right by with a couple of simple tools. Here's how.

How to Use Placeholders

Good writing happens when I stay relaxed and in the flow, but staying on task can be tricky. For example, let's say I am writing quickly and making progress, and I decide I want to include a story about a speaker I met at a local writers' conference. The problem is, I can't remember his name. Brown hair. Round wire-rimmed glasses. Green polo shirt. Can't remember his name.

In this moment, I face a critical choice.

Option One: I decide to Google the name of the conference and see if the speaker is listed in the program book. But while I am Googling, I find some fun new information about an upcoming conference I didn't know about, and it looks really good. I check my calendar and pencil in the dates; I check my savings account to see if I can afford the fees. Before I know it, I decide that I need another cup of coffee before I can continue, so I get up and go into the kitchen, and notice that it is surprisingly close to lunchtime. Just like that, my writing day is over and done. And I spent most of it chasing down a tiny detail that may or may not even end up in the book.

Option Two: I decide to hit caps lock on my computer, I type "**THAT GUY FROM THAT CONFERENCE GREEN POLO SHIRT**" and I keep writing. Because I am still in the flow, I manage to draft another thousand words before breaking for lunch. That is the power of a placeholder.

A placeholder is a word or phrase that stands in the gap until you have the time to circle back and fill in the details. The essential function of a placeholder is to create a reminder so you can stay in the flow, keep making progress, and come back to it at your leisure.

A placeholder might mark a name you can't remember or a specific date you need to check. I hit the caps lock button and write "NAME" or "DATE." A placeholder might also be a way to handle it when you can't quite find the right word. I *could* head over to the online thesaurus and scroll through it, trying to find the exact term I am looking for. But I know that once I exit my document, I am not likely to return to it any time soon. Instead, I write "THAT WORD THAT MEANS FRETTING" or "A SYNONYM FOR ACCURATE."

The same process of using placeholders works when I want to insert a quotation. Rather than hunting for it now, I write "THAT QUOTE FROM BALDWIN," and I keep drafting as fast as I can.

As I was writing this book, I wanted to include several personal stories. But since I am not good with numbers, I don't always remember *when* something happened. If you were to look at my early drafts, you would see a lot of sentences that use "NNN" as a placeholder for a specific number I need to look up later, such as "About NNN years ago," or "It took me NNN weeks," or "When I was in NNN grade," or "It was published in NNN."

There are many effective ways to indicate a placeholder. Some writers flag a placeholder with a searchable character such as * or ^. Some highlight it, use bold text, or change its color. Or they add a comment in the margin. Any of these will work if they help you quickly find your placeholders later. And stay doggedly on task for now.

Here's what I love about placeholders. They make sure I keep my seat in my chair and continue writing. They improve my accuracy by forcing me to come back and double-check details like dates and other specifics, rather than guessing or researching on the spot. And they let me avoid getting lost in the dictionary or thesaurus while searching for the perfect word.

But there's one more extremely helpful benefit: They also create "micro-tasks" for me to add to my to-do list. Micro-tasks are short, simple, self-contained tasks that I can complete in five minutes or less. Look up a quotation. Search for the name of that author. Find a synonym. Verify the date. These quick and easy tasks are really useful when I don't have much time to work on my project, or when the Muse is elusive, or my mind is elsewhere.

Write as fast as you can. Write as badly as you dare.

On a bad writing day, I can usually still muster enough focus to fill a few placeholders. And once I've done that, I often find that I can press on and add a few paragraphs—or even pages—to my draft. But the biggest benefit is this: Putting small tasks aside for another day means that for now, I can continue in the flow of drafting—writing fast, without stopping.

How to Use Scaffolding

Another great tool that helps me write with velocity is scaffolding. In construction, a scaffold is a temporary structure used to support workers and their equipment until the project is completed. Builders then remove the scaffolds once they have served their purpose. The same is true of a scaffold in writing. While a placeholder might mark a missing name, number, date, or elusive term, a scaffold is a note that you write to yourself. It may ask a question, critique a choice, or flag a concern. It creates a temporary reminder to return to later—but in the meantime, it empowers us to keep moving forward and keep on drafting.

Here's how it works. Let's say that as I am writing, I sense that I need an example to help clarify a point, but I can't think of a good one right now. So right in the text, I write "FIND A SPECIFIC EXAMPLE HERE." And I press on, drafting as fast as I can. Or let's say that I am concerned that the story I am telling is redundant. Rather than flipping back through the pages of my manuscript and trying to figure out why this feels so familiar, I write "DIDN'T YOU ALREADY COVER THIS IN CHAPTER TWO?" or "DOUBLE-CHECK: REDUNDANT?" Other scaffolding might say something like "PUT A NEW INTRODUCTION HERE," "TRANSITION NEEDED," or "FIND ONE MORE QUOTATION." And then I press on. If you prefer to write electronically, the comment feature on Word and Google is a lifesaver.

Other instructions can be helpful as I try to maintain velocity and keep my seat in the chair. I might express concerns about flow, or uncertainty about content, such as knowing that I need more of something, but I can't quite put my finger on what that is right now. I remind myself to do more research, refine terms, look for synonyms, double-check citations, add transitions, or make a host of other refinements later. But when I am drafting, I am trying to gallop through as much text as I possibly can. If I keep stopping to research facts, refine the text, or polish details, I'll lose my momentum. I won't get any writing done. Remember: Write as fast as you can. Write as badly as you dare.

Like placeholders, scaffolds also create micro-tasks I can take on during a ten or fifteen-minute block later in the day or week. Scaffolding may also represent places where I'm struggling and need to ask a friend or an editor to help or serve as a sounding board. In the meantime, this strategy allows me to produce as much text as I can during the time I've blocked out to write.

A warning. True story: When I was writing my dissertation, I got super frustrated with one section of the text. In the draft, I wrote the words, "This part THIN. Beef up your argument!"

Only I didn't notice that I left that scaffolding in place when I submitted my draft to my dissertation committee.

Did they see it? They didn't say anything, and I didn't ask, so I will never know. But whatever you do, make sure your placeholders and scaffolding are distinguished somehow from the main text—all caps, highlighted, marked by a double asterisk, etc.—to make sure they will *not* remain in your final draft.

Using placeholders and scaffolding keeps me moving forward and helps me make steady progress toward completing the first draft. Instead of writing a single paragraph, revising it, deleting half of it, writing a new sentence, and then deleting the whole section, I relax and keep moving forward. I write and keep writing, as quickly as I can and as badly as I dare.

Chapter 6 Summary
DRAFT

- Keep in mind that your goal when drafting is to get it down.
- Choose materials and tools that help you create, view, and share your work.
- Start anywhere: beginning, middle, or end.
- Write as quickly as you can.
- Write as badly as you dare.
- Use placeholders and scaffolding to help you maintain momentum.

The Big Idea

Writing is hard. Do what you can to make it easier.

Take a Step

What two or three tools—digital or analog, practical or inspirational—might enhance your writing space and help you stay focused? What supports you as you are working?

A Final Word

When you are drafting, your goal is to *get it down*. Later, you'll have the chance to *get it right* (revise) and then make it great (edit).

Chapter 7
PERSIST
Overcome Obstacles

There's a popular quote attributed to the journalist Roger Simon that declares, "There is no such thing as writer's block." Simon explains it this way: "My father drove a truck for forty years. And never once did he wake up in the morning and say, 'I have truck driver's block today. I am not going to work.'"

It's a funny story, but you know what? Simon is wrong. There are many tasks that I can complete whether I feel like it or not: wash some dishes, tidy my desk, shop for groceries. These tasks do not require much focus or motivation. But writing well is not this kind of task.

One of the things I love about writing is how engaging it is. It demands my closest attention, my best focus, and my highest level of energy. One thing I hate about writing is that it demands my closest attention, my best focus, and my highest level of energy. Depending on the day, it can either feel like total magic or pulling teeth.

There are moments, though, when we are carried along in a flow state, staying "in the zone," or "locking in." You know the feeling—you suddenly realize you have been so completely immersed in a task that you have lost all track of time, and you can see that the work you've been doing truly reflects your best abilities.

Cal Newport calls this "deep work," and he claims it is the "superpower of the 21st century." I agree. Unfortunately, deep work is becoming increasingly rare. We face more distractions than ever before. We are more connected to the world around us; therefore, there can be constant interruptions when we are trying to get stuff done. It's very difficult to turn off the flow of information coming from the technology we own and from the constant stream of information pulsing through our minds.

However, deep work is also rare because we perceive it as "pure luck" or something totally out of our control. We love the compelling presence of inspiration and wish there was a way to flick a switch and make it happen.

True, it isn't entirely within our control to turn on and off at will. However, many factors can help us achieve a state of deep work and then stay there. This is the secret of prolific writers: They aren't necessarily more talented, less busy, or better at sitting still. Rather, they have mastered the variables that contribute to this kind of focus. They have learned to buckle down and then guard against distractions. You can do it, too.

When You Start to Lose Momentum

Some days, the Muse fails to show up. Inspiration is in short supply. Fatigue and distraction take center stage. Real life gets noisy, heavy, or harrowing. Or the right word, key phrase, best illustration, or fresh insight *refuses* to come to mind. It happens. And that's okay. Here are some ideas to help you keep your seat in your chair on days like that.

Change the Task

While the main task at hand might be drafting, some days, I'm just too tired, angry, frustrated, and distracted. Rather than throw in the towel for the day, I ask: What tasks can I do right now that will contribute something to my writing, even indirectly?

Maybe I can *loop back* to the gathering stage: I can read something related to my topic or maybe read something about writing. I can listen to podcasts that focus on creativity or the creative process. I can read or listen to interviews with writers.

Or maybe my best strategy for today is to *leap forward* into detail work. I can look up and correct my citations or proofread my bibliography. I can research characters, visit locations, or rework dialogue. I can gather examples or search for quotations. I can make lists or outlines of my main points and check for balance and flow. I can check the format and make corrections. This flexible structure is the beauty of the Pathway Approach.

A few days ago, I was feeling listless. Uninspired. I decided to leap forward and play around with the back cover blurb and the authors' descriptions of this book. I went to Canva and designed a mock cover. I also played around with the headings and layout for the Table of Contents. I'm a visual learner, and fiddling with visual elements often helps me picture the final goal. While my conscious mind makes design decisions, my subconscious clarifies the meaning of my message. It may look like I'm wasting time, but I know from experience that this kind of visual play refocuses my attention and settles my soul. It primes the pump for writing.

What works for you? There are so many possibilities. What is essential is that you keep your head in the game and then inch just a little closer to the finish line.

Change the Format

I draft on a computer. Most writers do. But when I get stuck, especially when I lose track of my structure or feel fuzzy about what I need to do next, I resort to ink and paper. I print out my pages, and I revise and edit by hand. Moving from the computer screen to the typed page and working with a pen rather than a keyboard often refreshes my ability to refocus my attention and stay on task.

For a large project, like a book, I print pages periodically and put them in a three-ring binder. It is hard for me to hold the whole project in my mind at one time; a printed copy helps. Flipping through the physical pages helps me gain a fresh perspective. In addition, my binder is portable, so I can take it with me to a new location. And I find that there are times when drawing visual outlines, handwriting paragraphs or dialogues, line editing, and similar tasks are easier and more fun when I am working with colored markers, red pens, and highlighters. And sticky notes. Always sticky notes.

I'm not giving up my laptop anytime soon. But for me, resorting to analog tools can be a great help in maintaining momentum, especially on long-term projects. Austin Kleon is one of my favorite creativity gurus, and he has the right idea: "While I love my computer, I think computers have robbed us of the feeling that we're actually making things. Instead, we're just typing keys and clicking mouse buttons." Find ways to connect with your work in tangible ways.

Stretch, Move, Breathe

Earlier, we discussed how our natural biorhythms make us more productive writers at certain times of the day. Biorhythms also play a role in sustaining our momentum.

I believe that a lot of the time, we don't actually have a "creative block." We are just hungry. Headachy. Restless. Or sad. Or maybe we've just been sitting in that creaky office chair too long. Maybe my body is just tired of sitting, so my back aches, and my left hand feels a little numb.

Often, the secret to resetting our mental state is to attend to our physical state. Are you weary? Stand and stretch. Distracted? Go grab a snack. Frustrated? Sit in the sunshine. Pet your cat. Take a shower. Stand barefoot in the grass. Grab some water. Stretch. Do a few push-ups. Anything that helps you reset.

In Gary Provost's helpful book *100 Ways to Improve Your Writing*, Tip #13 is "Touch Your Toes." Provost explains:

> If your toes are too far away to touch, then stretch your arms or dance or jump up and down. Whatever. James Michener actually goes into physical training like a boxer before he begins a book, so the least you can do is take a few deep breaths, put your pulse rate in second gear, and deliver a supply of oxygen to the brain.

Finding it hard to find the words? Take a short break and get moving.

Change Your Location

Sitting at a desk, standing at a table, leaning against a pile of pillows in bed. Writers write in many different places and work under many different circumstances. Our location and our posture can help or hinder our progress.

Experiment with writing in different rooms. Discover whether staying in the same place helps you stay focused, or whether it helps to move from the desk to the floor, to the couch, to the dining room table at regular intervals. Try working outside—a park, backyard, public garden, arboretum—and enjoy some fresh air. If you usually write at home, get up and out. Visit your local café or public library. A new environment may generate new ideas.

I have an office at home with a desktop computer, and that is where I do most of my writing. However, I find different locations sustain me during different phases of the writing process. I tend to prewrite while I sit on the couch with a legal pad and a pile of books. It is the best place for me to jot notes, draw visual outlines, and write out lists of questions. I draft on my desktop computer, sometimes at the dining room table, or at my desk at work. There is a quiet corner of my local library that works well when I need to dig deep, set aside a big block of time, and concentrate on a complex task like drafting.

Once I have a working draft, I almost always edit my text in a noisy, busy, crowded location. I have a favorite table at a local coffee shop where the noise and bustle help when I am struggling to stay focused through a slow, sleepy afternoon.

Writing in public and seeing people come and go around me is energizing. Writing when there are a lot of other people around me has another benefit: It gets me in touch with my audience. I start thinking, "How would this section be different if I were to write it just for that person sitting at the next table?" or "Would that person relate to this example, understand this term, be encouraged by this story, find it easy to picture that character?"

Create a Deadline

Nothing is more catalyzing for a writer than a deadline. I received an email from my publisher a few days ago. "I'd like to see your progress on Chapter Seven," it said. Suddenly, evenings, mornings, and all of my weekends were blocked off for writing. Suddenly, I was wide awake, completely focused, and writing as fast as I could.

If you don't have a publisher or professor to give you a deadline, the structure of a self-imposed deadline can work wonders. For fiction writers, joining the NaNoWriMo 2.0 (National Novel Writing Month) finish-your-manuscript-in-a-month challenge can be a godsend. Or perhaps you and a friend can hold each other accountable for your daily writing goals.

I know writers who have taken an easy, effective tip from runners. Those trying to build a habit of running every day text their daily mileage to a small group of fellow runners. Just the number: 4.6 miles, 8.1 miles, 10.45 miles, and so on. Following this model, some writers will text their daily word count or post it on social media: 345 words, 1,243 words. A little friendly competition goes a long way.

One quick caveat: Not all writers function well with deadlines. For some, the stress can stunt their creativity or even *cause* writer's block. However, the structure of reasonable, incremental deadlines, combined with a bit of accountability, is exactly what many writers need to ensure they are making progress toward their goal.

Try a Timer

Many of us find that the first twenty minutes of a writing session are the most difficult—the time when we are the most distracted and therefore, the most tempted to flee. For this reason, Joseph Bentz has a strategy he calls "The Battle of the First 20 Minutes." He described the battle to me this way:

> I set a strict rule for myself that no matter what, I am not allowed to do anything else during those first twenty minutes. I do not demand much productivity during those minutes, but winning the battle means I sit there and do not give in to other temptations. I can read what I wrote the day before, read notes I've written to myself, stare at the screen, peck out a sentence, but nothing else. For me, once I do this, my mind gradually takes on the writing world, and the flow begins.

If you can stay put for the first twenty minutes or so, you are much more likely to settle into a productive writing day. Try starting your writing time with a twenty-minute timer to keep you locked in.

And if you write for a while and then get tangled up in overthinking, a "writing sprint" may give you the push you need. This means setting a timer and writing nonstop until it goes off. No slowing down, no evaluating, no editing. The goal is to write as many words as possible. The self-created pressure keeps you focused, and the act of writing without overthinking often generates acceleration for the task ahead.

You might also try the Pomodoro Technique. Francesco Cirillo developed it in the late 1980s and named it after a tomato-shaped kitchen timer popular at the time. The strategy is simple and surprisingly effective. Choose a task, or a set of tasks, and set a timer for twenty-five minutes (one "pomodoro"). Work exclusively on that one task until the timer rings. If you are interrupted or switch to a different task, the pomodoro is considered void. You must start over.

When the timer goes off, take a five-minute break. Stretch, take a drink of water, grab a snack. Once you complete four pomodoros, take a longer break, typically twenty or thirty minutes.

My students often report that the Pomodoro Technique helps enhance their concentration (short bursts help focus), overcome procrastination (short sprints feel doable), prevent burnout (mandatory breaks help them avoid mental fatigue), and build good habits. Some of them experiment by randomly changing the length of the intervals; others determine the length of their interval by the nature of the task at hand.

There are apps and websites designed to facilitate this technique. Some are specifically designed for writers. Some have visual progress trackers. Some gamify the challenge of focusing. One app grows a virtual tree, which will die if you start looking at your phone instead of working. *You don't want to let the little tree die, do you?* Take advantage of timers and tools designed to help rein in your attention so you can focus on what matters.

Put Distractions in Their Place

Whether I am typing, handwriting, or dictating, there are two things I always keep nearby: a pen and a pile of post-it notes. It is my favorite way to handle distractions. I know that while I write, my mind will whisper, "buy dog food, call Linda, schedule that oil change." Or all of a sudden, I will have brilliant ideas for a different book, another article, or maybe a whole new project.

If I give in to these voices, I get derailed. If I try to ignore them, they stay in my head, straining my focus. Instead, I let them out. I write each as a reminder on a sticky note, and then I physically put it aside. The pen captures the reminders. The notes hold them for me until it is time to deal with them. In the meantime, my attention is free to stay focused on my writing.

MAGIC TRICK
Prepare Tomorrow's Task Today

There is one technique that has helped me more than any other in maintaining momentum and getting my writing done. It has guided me more than any other magic trick as I have struggled to gather my thoughts, complete my first rough draft, and then revise, edit, and proofread. Like many of my most helpful writing habits, I learned this from Don Murray: I prepare tomorrow's writing task today.

Here's what that looks like for me. As I end each day's writing session, I do everything I can to prepare for what's next. I want to work hard to set the stage. I want stepping back into my project to be as smooth and easy as putting on my old, familiar slippers.

First, I set up my space. I clear the clutter. I assemble any needed materials, including the books I know I will need, along with any articles, web links, or printouts. I collect my tools, like highlighter pens and sharpened pencils.

Next, I write down a list of very simple, specific, and concrete steps to take as I start my next writing day: Run a grammar check on pages 10–15. Look up that quotation about rough drafts from Paul J. Silvia, add the citation, and double-check it for accuracy. Revise the story about Mike.

Sometimes? I deliberately type a paraagraphf ful of mistaadk. On porpice. Then I kan harddley wait to get back to the document the next day just so I can FIX THEM! Or I'll stop in the middle of a sentence or partway through the transcription of a quotation. It's painful, but effective. It works every time, like magic.

Finally, as I finish up my writing for the day, I decide which specific task will be the *easiest possible* starting point, and I write it on a sticky note that says, "Start here."

The next time I sit down to write, I look at my note, and I start with this one small task. The decision has already been made for me. I know exactly what to do. And I have all the materials right in front of me that I will need to complete that one simple, specific, concrete task. After that, I am primed for more challenging tasks. Once I get going, the topic, the project, or my affection for my readers pulls me through.

The Goal? A Rough First Draft

At this point, you have been writing rapidly, getting your thoughts down on the page. Perhaps you're working your way through the last few chapters or going back to draft that section you skipped earlier. The goal of the drafting stage is to complete a rough first draft, the "down draft." But because there is always more to do, it can be tricky to identify this milestone.

What signs can we use to discern when a first draft is done? Here are some indicators:

- You have greater clarity about what you are trying to say.
- You know roughly where you'll end up.
- You have identified the major sections or plot points that will guide the reader from beginning to middle to end.
- You are running low on ideas about what else to include.
- You realize that you need to take a step back to renew your perspective.

Overall, the first draft is complete when all major parts of the work are *drafted*, even if they are not equally *developed*.

But wait. Are there gaps? Clumsy wording? Problems, inconsistencies, wordiness, gaps, and redundancies? Good. That's good. You are right where you need to be. You have established the framework—ideas that once only existed in your head have been put into words on the page and pulled together into one document. All of this brings you closer to your ultimate goal: delivering a powerful message to the reader who needs to hear it.

Now, get ready for PART THREE.

Chapter 7 Summary
PERSIST

- Maintain momentum by changing the task: drafting, outlining, researching, designing, running a spell-checker, writing a blurb, and designing a cover all count as progress.
- Maintain momentum by changing the format: Try a new font, a different font size, single spacing instead of double spacing, or print it out.
- Stay energized by moving, stretching, and taking breaks.
- Try a change of location, from the desk to the dining room table, or from home to a coffee shop. This can renew your perspective, invite better ideas, and reset your concentration.
- Deadlines, timers, and apps can help you focus.
- Deal with distractions by writing yourself a note and putting it aside while you stay focused on your work. Attend to these other matters another time.
- Stay on track by preparing tomorrow's task today.

The Big Idea
When you are struggling, don't give up. No matter how uninspired you feel, there is still a lot you can do to make progress.

Take a Step
Select two or three strategies that would help you to keep going on a day when you don't want to write. List them and put them somewhere where they will remind you of what's possible.

A Final Word
Recognize that completing a first draft, as raggedy as it may be, is an extraordinary accomplishment.

PART THREE (Finally!) Get It Done

What makes me happy is rewriting. In the first draft, you get your ideas and your theme clear. If you are using some kind of metaphor, you get that established, and certainly you have to know where you're coming out. But the next time through it's like cleaning house, getting rid of all the junk, getting things in the right order, tightening things up. I like the process of making writing neat.
Ellen Goodman

A completed draft. Now that's worth celebrating. But often, close on the heels of finishing a draft, we are assaulted with nagging questions: Is it good enough? Is it really ready? Is there anything that I can do to refine it, bring it to the next level, take it up a notch? Can I transform what I've written from good to great?

Emphatically yes! In PART THREE, we'll focus on rewriting: how to strengthen, improve, and refine what you've written.

Each of the next three chapters will have a specific focus—revising, editing, and proofreading, respectively. People often use these terms interchangeably; however, I'll show you that each step focuses on a different task. The Pathway Approach defines each of these three concepts in a very specific way.

Revising: Addressing the big picture; adjusting what you have to say and how it's structured

Editing: Focusing on sentences and words; seeking clarity and grace

Proofreading: The task of finding mistakes and fixing them

You've already done the hardest part. You started strong, and you maintained momentum. You are almost there. Now, let's get this done.

Chapter 8
REVISE
Rework the Big Picture

At this point, you've finished your draft. Well, it's not *finished*, not quite yet. But in the process of writing, you've developed a much clearer idea of what you want to say. You've established your key content. You know where the piece begins, and you have a good idea where it ends. You've set the tone and established the voice. Your understanding of your topic has deepened. And you're right where you need to be. As Bernard Malamud says, "First drafts are for learning what your novel or story is about."

He's exactly right. First drafts are for learning. Picture the draft as a pencil sketch. You've found your focal point and shaped your boundary lines. The main features are there, and they are roughly in the right place. But to progress from rough sketch to finished work of art, there are still specifics to add, descriptions to refine, and details to correct.

Writing is discovery. Now: Rewriting is enriching, enhancing, and refining.

When you sit down and reread something you have written, the first things to jump out at you will be the small stuff, such as pesky typos, awkward phrasing, and clunky format issues. They may cry out for your attention: "Look here! Fix me! Focus on me! I'm so easy to fix!" But if you give in, you'll find yourself buried in details, spending hours niggling over this and fussing over that. What's the use of fixing every typo on the page when you may discover that the page needs to be entirely rewritten or perhaps even cut out?

There will be a time for correcting each detail, but revision is not that time. *Revising is the radical process of adjusting big-picture issues*. It means taking a step back and doing everything you can to see the whole, entire project with fresh eyes. Revision means asking overarching questions, like this:

> **Structure**: Have I put everything in the best possible order? Is the amount of space I devote to each part of it proportionate to its importance? Think: Move it.
>
> **Focus**: Is my main point or narrative thread strong and clear? Does every part of the piece—every scene, every example, every section, every chapter, every sentence—accomplish important work, giving value to my reader and contributing something substantial to my main point? Think: Delete it.
>
> **Content**: Is anything missing—are there gaps where my reader will falter or leaps where the storyline crumbles, or my points don't connect? Think: Add to it.

The focus for revision is global. Think *big*. Address the major issues. Scrutinize how each section conveys your central message and serves your reader.

I often tell writers that revision is architecture, not interior decorating. It's knocking down walls, not adding a coat of paint. Or, as Donald M. Murray used to tell us, "The proper tool of revision is not a touch-up brush. It is a *chainsaw*." For the sake of our project, we shift our mindset from the generous Creator to finicky Critic. At this stage, we ask, ask, and

"Revising is a radical process of adjusting big-picture issues.

ask again: What can I do to take this to the next level? What changes, big and small, will make this clearer, stronger, and more compelling? How can I take every aspect of this from weak to strong, from good to great?

These questions and more will vary depending on the genre and type of writing. For example, at this stage, fiction writers will want to reconsider their point of view, pacing, and foreshadowing. They will assess the overall narrative arc. They will also take a close look at character development. These are decisions that affect the entire work.

This chapter explains how you can see your draft with a fresh perspective, and then adjust your structure and your content to clarify your message and engage your reader.

"Re-See" Your Draft

To figure out what we need to move, or delete, or add to our text, we need a fresh perspective. This can be tricky when we've been staring at these same pages for hours, months, or even years. We tend to look at the text and see what we *meant*. It can be really hard to read what we *actually said* and then evaluate it objectively.

A few years ago, Abigail was working with María, an author who wanted to adapt her play script into a fantasy novel. For months, they collaborated on the challenging task of translating all the energy of the stage production onto the page—from the sibling banter to the sounds of the rainforest to the songs that carry the story's themes. They spent hours, weeks, and months developing character profiles and researching the folktales that informed the story.

They thought the manuscript was nearly finished. But when they brought in another team member to read it, it became clear that while the book was full of excellent material, the plot was still not holding together. It opened quickly with action and mystery, but the larger narrative arc was fuzzy—more episodic than cohesive. The key character motivations were not always clear, and the magic system that underlined the story was underdeveloped.

Turns out, the story wasn't even close to done; it needed to be entirely reworked. This realization felt like a swift punch to the gut for author and editor alike.

To them, the most shocking part was that they had been immersed in the writing for months and hadn't seen this. In reality, it was *because* they had been so immersed in the work together that they didn't see it. And they didn't immediately see how to fix it either. They needed to re-see the draft to discover what was working, what wasn't, and exactly how to move forward.

Perhaps you've had a similar experience. Maybe you've also gotten to the "end" of a long project only to be told you weren't anywhere close. Here are some strategies to help you see your work afresh and become better at reading your own drafts.

Take a Break

Whether you are feeling the rush of inspiration or working hard under a tight deadline, it may be tempting to jump straight from drafting to revising or from revising to editing. However, you'll accomplish more if you can find a way to disengage before revising. This is what Abigail and María did next. They took a couple of months to get over the initial shock and get some distance from order of events that had become so familiar they seemed logical and inevitable, even when they weren't.

Taking a break gives us the fresh perspective we need to identify blind spots. When we've been deep in the material for so long, we begin to make lots of intuitive leaps that do not always make it to the page. When we go back a couple of hours, days, weeks, or even months later, we can see our work with a new perspective and fresh possibilities. We can recognize gaps, redundancies, assumptions, and clunky word choices we were previously blind to. We may also see bigger possibilities we were once too close to notice.

Taking time to pause—even for a short time—allows us to switch gears in a way that is not simply metaphorical. It refers to a real change that happens in our neural networks. That's because different parts of our brains are engaged as we focus on different aspects of the writing process. One part is activated when we create text, that is, while we are busy drafting, explaining, composing, and discovering new ideas. However, a different part of our brain is engaged when we reflect, evaluate, and critique. When we pause between stages, we literally transfer energy from one part of our brain to another, allowing us to engage a different set of skills. Besides refreshing our energy as we adapt to a new challenge, taking a pause helps us make important shifts between the writing and the rewriting stages.

Ray Bradbury famously claimed that when he finished a story, he put it in a drawer for a year. For a year! I don't have that kind of time, and I suspect that you don't, either. But think back. Can you remember a time when you stumbled across an old poem or story, a paper for a class, or an old article you wrote for a blog? When you looked at it again, months or years later, it is as if the flaws were highlighted with a neon marker. Like many writers, I find it painful to reread something once I've published it. The shortcomings are just so painfully obvious once I've stepped away from the work.

That's why it is important to take a break and disengage from time to time. Take a day or two, if you can. Even a student with a paper due at midnight could pause to stand up and walk around for a short five minutes. When I was in the midst of comprehensive exams, I would pause at the end of each essay, close my eyes, and take a minute to focus on deep breathing before I went back and reviewed my answer.

Taking a break doesn't have to be long or elaborate. *Any* pause gives you time to regroup, shift your mindset, reset your focus, and then start fresh. Your work will be far better for it.

Change the Text

A pause brings perspective. But you can also re-see your work by changing the way you're physically accustomed to looking at it.

Studies in human-computer interaction show that when we change the visual formatting of text, the patterns in our eye movement change. We may speed through, then regress and reread, and then slow down and linger on particular words and phrases. This means that with a different format, we perceive the text in a new way; the form draws our focus to elements we may not have noticed before.

Writers can use this to their advantage. If you are working in a word processor, consider changing the font or font size. Change the spacing from single to double, or from double to single, or change the margins from standard to narrow or extra-wide. My friend David always starts his revision process by shifting to a sans-serif font, 9-point type, single-space text with narrow margins. This allows him to take in the big picture of his prose in very big gulps. New aspects of your draft (strengths and weaknesses) become crystal clear as these kinds of visual changes reveal them.

Change the Mode

Just as changing the visual format helps us process text more effectively, so does changing the mode. Are you working on the computer? Print it out. Working on a handwritten draft? Type it up. Or record yourself reading it aloud and listen to how it sounds.

When I am nearing the end of the revision process, I often create a mock-up that echoes the way my text will look in its final form. An article takes on the shape of the magazine or journal where it will appear. A book manuscript gets formatted in the 5.5 x 8.5 or 6 x 9-inch size that the book pages will take when published. Seeing it reformatted helps me identify problems in proportion, transitions, pacing, or development.

Read It Fast

You've changed the text and shifted the mode. Here's another way to get a clearer sense of what you have written: Read it fast. Journalist Chip Scanlan summarizes his process of gaining a new perspective on his drafts this way:

> Hit the print button on whatever you have and take it downstairs, outside, anywhere outside of the newsroom and read it first quickly. Don't mark it up. Just read it fast like a reader might, groggy at the breakfast table. Then take a pen and this time, start making marks in the margin.

Change it up. Print it out. Read it fast. When I wrote *The Company They Keep*, my first book about Lewis and Tolkien, I wanted to get this big-picture view of the entire three-hundred-page manuscript. I printed it out, put the pages into a three-ring notebook, and went on a weekend writing retreat.

On the first morning, I got up extra early and read through the whole thing in one day, marking places that seemed slow, sections that felt out of sequence, redundant passages, and ideas that lurched awkwardly from one concept to another. Reading the entire book straight through in one sitting revealed the overall structure. I wanted this nonfiction, academic book to have a strong narrative arc, and this helped me see the big picture—main points and minor points; rising action and falling action; the introduction of conflict and its resolution.

I got up extra early on the second morning and read through the whole thing again. But this time, I started with the last chapter and worked my way through the book from the final chapter to the first. I read very quickly, and I tried to pay extra attention to when and how specific terms and key concepts were introduced and defined.

When I got back home, I started revising in short bursts, informed by the global perspective I had gained from the retreat.

Mark It Up

As you read through your draft, mark it up and keep big-picture questions in mind. Is some of this stuff redundant? Are there gaps? Do I need to change the order of the material? Do I need to unpack a general statement by adding clearer information and maybe an example or two? How is the pace: Is it too slow? Or does a key detail fly by too quickly? Does it feel like a cohesive whole, or are there lapses in tone and form? Is there too much going on? In fact, would it work better if it were broken down into several different works, two books instead of one, or three articles in a series rather than one overwhelming piece?

Ask good questions, and take notes as you go, keeping the big picture in mind.

MAGIC TRICK

Scissors and Tape

I was in my office for a scheduled one-on-one writing conference. I had read my student's six-page draft in advance, and I was struck by the fact that the first and third parts of her argument were virtually identical. When I tried to explain this to her, it was clear that I wasn't getting through. She simply did not understand what I was telling her.

So I pulled out a roll of tape and a pair of scissors. Her eyes grew wide. I removed the staple, cut the headers off the top of each page, and taped her entire paper together, the top of one page connecting to the bottom of another, like a scroll.

We sat on the floor of my office with her paper unfurled on the floor between us, reviewing it as one long, continuous essay. I pointed to the content of Part One. We compared it to the content of Part Three. Then I took out the scissors. I cut out Part One and added it to the end of Part Three. The essay clicked into place. Suddenly, simply by moving that material, we made her argument stronger and much more cohesive. She just needed help seeing the big picture, getting the birds-eye view, and discovering how the different sections of her paper related to each other. It was magic.

Drafting on a computer has a million advantages. It's fast, legible, editable, checkable, and shareable. It is really easy to duplicate it: Make a copy and then experiment with radical changes, saving the original in case you want to go back to your original vision. It is easy to store backups for safekeeping, easy to work on the same document from multiple locations, and easy to see the effects of different fonts, layouts, and other design elements on the message you want to convey.

But the downside of working on a computer is this: The writer sees roughly two hundred words at a time. So while it is certainly easy to draft, save, edit, and share, it is also very easy to write in short bits and completely lose track of how all the parts work together. Is everything in the right order? Are the proportions right? Is there a balance and consistency in the use of quotations, number of stories, examples, key terms, and concepts? You can't answer those questions when all you are looking at is one small, isolated chunk of text.

And the fact is, your reader is not going to be limited to a mere two hundred words at a stretch. You are expecting them to embark on a journey. To do that, you need to understand the big picture. Scissors and tape can be enormously helpful in the process.

Next time you're feeling lost in the weeds of revision, try printing out your text. Tape the pages together, end-to-end. Then cut it into pieces by scene or topic, section or subsection. Lay the pieces out on the floor and experiment; re-see all the new—and potentially better—ways that your paragraphs might find their flow.

MOVE IT
Strengthen Your Structure

With a renewed focus and a fresh perspective, you can begin to see your writing in a new way. One valuable way to begin revising is to consider the structure. Imagine seeing your work from an airplane window. Or as a blueprint laid out on a single page. What are the major sections? Are they defined by parts, chapters, or plot points? And what transitions connect one place to the next? Is there a clear pathway for the reader to move from beginning to middle to end without getting confused or bored? Should Chapter 5 become the new Chapter 1? Should the scenes be re-sequenced to heighten the impact?

It can be tricky for you as a writer to get this perspective when you're so close to your work, but refining your structure is an essential skill. Not only does it clarify your reader's experience, but it can also give you a checklist for what to delete or add to your text.

See Your Structure

How do you gain insight into the structure of your work? One way to do that is with a reverse outline. While an outline generally is used to map out what you *plan* to write, a reverse outline is when you create a map of what you have *already* written. It needn't be fancy. Start by creating a Table of Contents for what you have, then add more details to show the components within each section. A standard outline may be useful, but an informal list may work just as well. The word processor I am using as I write this allows me to label the headings and subheadings of the text and displays these headers along the left side of the document. Creating a quick scratch outline, or even just copying your document and deleting everything but the headings, can help you to see the overall infrastructure of your work.

I am a visual learner, so I often prefer what are called "visual outlines," sometimes called graphic organizers, mind maps, or sketch notes. Unlike a linear, text-based outline, a visual outline works more like a flowchart. It identifies different ideas by using shapes like triangles, circles, and squares to map out main points, supporting points, and details. A quick internet search will suggest dozens of examples of how to use visual outlines to organize information. Visual outlines help me to picture the relationship between the main point, minor claims, and supporting details more clearly.

However you choose to create a more visual and dynamic snapshot of your work, seeing your work represented on one single page or image helps you to make good decisions about the best order for your ideas.

Another helpful way to reveal your structure? Use highlighter pens: Color-code main points, transitions, supporting details, examples, and illustrations. Author Austin Kleon offers important advice on getting a fresh vision of your work. In his book *Steal Like an Artist*, he advocates using both analog and digital tools:

> I have two desks in my office—one is "analog" and one is "digital." The analog desk has nothing but markers, pens, pencils, paper, index cards, and newspaper. … Take $10, go to the school supply aisle of your local store, and pick up some paper, pens, and sticky notes. When you come back to your analog station, pretend it's craft time. Scribble on paper, cut it up, and tape the pieces back together. … Pin things on the walls and look for patterns. Spread things around your space and sort through them.

Kleon concludes, "Once you start getting your ideas, then you can move over to your digital station and use the computer to help you execute and publish them." Using both digital and analog tools can engage both mind and imagination. Kinesthetic learners have the most to gain from this hands-on approach. At their best, these tools help us see the text in new ways and then suggest new strategies to help us connect with our readers.

Review Your Sequence

As Abigail and María dove back into María's manuscript, sequence was one of the major items they reviewed. The original draft opened with a bullying scene, then proceeded with a straightforward quest. The siblings were transported to their home island of Puerto Rico, where they met a talking parrot and then set out to find a mysterious Sleeping Giant to save the island and find their way home.

Themes and mentions of grief were woven through the story, but this sequence failed to capture the fact that the story was supposed to be set in motion by the death of the children's father and the ways they attempted to cope with this tragedy. They re-sequenced the story, starting with a scene depicting the grief the children felt after losing their father, making the emotional stakes clear from the start. As a result, the magic no longer felt incidental; it gained a direct connection to their father's past—the central force driving the story, clarifying motivation, and unifying the plot toward a crescendo of healing and resilience for the family and island alike.

The events were largely the same, but a change in the sequence solved nearly all the narrative problems at once. The book went on to win recognition from the Independent Book Publishers Association and the International Latino Book Awards.

Ed Catmull, cofounder of Pixar, describes a similar revision process as the team worked on *Finding Nemo*. In an early draft of the script, members of the team reported that Nemo's father Marlin was impossible to sympathize with because he was so overbearing and irritating. The solution was to restructure the story. Rather than unveiling Marlin's tragic loss of his wife and children late in the story, they changed the sequence and made it into the opening scene. By placing Marlin's loss front and center, the viewer immediately empathized with him. The emotional stakes at the start of the film set the foundation for everything that would follow, including the film's place as one of Pixar's most beloved movies to date.

If you're writing fiction, consider this: What needs to be established up-front so that my reader will inhabit the world I'm creating? What do they need to know for the emotional beats and big reveals to hit home?

If you're writing nonfiction, consider this: What does my reader need to know first, second, and third? What steps might they need to complete before they can proceed to other steps? What new information might be easier for them to accept before introducing something more challenging?

Fiction or nonfiction, the sequence you select creates the path for their transformation.

Balance Your Proportions

As we have seen, sequence asks if everything has been presented in the best order. Proportion asks a different question: Does the length of each section match its importance? If you spend a long time explaining a minor point, the reader is going to think it's a major point. If you breeze through a major point, the reader is not going to realize how significant it is, and they may be confused or lost when you build upon it later. Don't skimp, and don't hide the lead. I was working with one of my undergraduates this semester. I read twenty-three pages of his twenty-five-page term paper before I found his thesis statement. To make matters worse, it was buried in the middle of a paragraph.

Check to see if you have given your key ideas the most space on the page. Are the main points elaborated? Did you keep incidental details short? In your novel, the central conflict between your characters might be eight pages long; background descriptions should be much shorter. In your memoir, the most telling aspects of your story may get three examples; the minor points get only one.

In addition, use structural cues to communicate to the reader what is significant by lingering longer, elaborating further, and inviting them to spend more time. As Annie Dillard says, "If something in your narrative or poem is important, give it proportional space. I mean, actual inches. The reader has to spend time with a subject to care about it. Don't shy away from your big scenes; stretch them out."

Use the following tests to check your proportions. Compare the length of your major sections. Write down the word counts of your chapters and check the length of subsections. Ask yourself if each chapter of your novel is about the same length. Does each one of your points in a four-part argument run roughly the same number of pages? Are illustrations and quotations distributed evenly? Do the introductions and conclusions of each main section clearly signal the transition from one idea to another? If you find something out of balance, consider moving material in or out of that section.

When the structure is balanced, the work gains cohesion. It feels purposeful and consistent. It gives the reader a sense of security when they know how the parts of a work will be structured. And it makes it far easier to track the main points, follow the story, and feel confident that everything is moving toward a worthwhile destination.

DELETE IT
Refine Your Focus

When you look back over your draft, you may notice that some pieces don't seem to fit anymore; some sections have duplicates; some parts are way longer than others with no rhyme or reason. You may realize that some parts of the work are interesting or well-written, but they no longer relate to your point at all.

Now is the time to cut out anything that doesn't belong.

An illustration may be helpful here. In my neighborhood, they have been constructing a large trestle for a light rail commuter train. The entire overpass has been shrouded in a web of metal beams and wooden supports, and it's been like that for months and months. But soon, the work will be finished, and they will pull those extraneous beams away and allow the steel and concrete structure to stand on its own. Similarly, we may write a great deal of material for ourselves during the drafting process. It takes time and experimentation to figure out what we want to say and the best way to say it. But our readers don't need all that extra scaffolding. They want to see the finished product, with all the temporary props cleared away.

How do you decide what to cut? How do you distinguish a temporary support from a critical pillar? Some writers review their manuscripts by asking, "What parts do I like?" or "What parts are really good?" Don't do it. Both of those questions get a writer into trouble. The first question can lead a writer to focus on their personal tastes and ignore the reader's needs and concerns. The second question can lead a writer to favor those passages that are beautifully written but ultimately irrelevant to the work as a whole.

What is a better question to ask? This: "What is working in this draft?"

Writer and editor William Zinsser says, "With each rewrite I try to make what I have written tighter, stronger, and more precise, eliminating every element that is not doing useful work." If you were to listen in on a group of experienced writers who are reading and critiquing each other's work, you would hear the same language again and again. They would *not* say, "This part is good" or "This part is bad." They would say, "This isn't working."

Good writing serves your message—the one thing you most want your reader to walk away with. We crave focus. As Donald M. Murray explains:

> In writing my column and my textbooks, my poems and my novels, my essays and my articles, I could only say one thing. Everything in the piece of writing had to lead to or away from that message. Focus makes sure that one meaning is emphasized, and once that is established everything in the piece of writing must support and develop that meaning.

Murray uses strong language here—*only* one thing, *everything* in the piece. Find your focus. Clarify your message. I am convinced that this is some of the best advice a writer can receive.

You must test each sentence and ask the hardest of all hard questions: What is my point, and does this contribute to my point? I think of how often I have heard a sermon that starts with a joke and meanders through four or five interesting observations before closing with a Bible verse and a prayer. I think of how many lectures I have heard that make a series of observations with no more to connect them than a vague, general topic. I think of family members who start telling a story about what happened to their kid at school and somehow end up talking about a conversation they had with a neighbor about rising prices at the grocery store, never to return to their initial point.

In contrast, how refreshing it is when a speaker or writer defines their message and then stays on track. Remember: Your readers are hungry for focus. If I offer a random list—tire, Persian, groundhog, nineteen, pencil, Julia—it is not only harder to remember, but it's also much harder to listen to. By nature, we love cohesion.

Every sentence has a job to do. And all of it, every bit of it, must serve your reader. Remember, your first draft is what you need to say; your final draft is what your reader needs to hear. Revision should focus on engaging their attention and anticipating their needs.

Find your focus. Think about your reader. Then challenge yourself. Can you cut 10%? Most prose pieces work far better when you do. Can you make even deeper cuts? One writer I know strives to shorten her work by 40% and finds that when her writing is lean and strong, it has a much greater impact. I was recently asked to cut a 2,300-word academic lecture into a 1,400-word article for a magazine. It was *hard.* And the result was so worth it.

If you are reviewing your draft and are unsure what to cut, the following are a few suggestions.

Shorten the Introduction

The material we may need to write for ourselves as we warm up may not help our readers. Think of those essays that begin with long rambling discourses about how they first got interested in their subject. Or—a pet peeve of mine—those blog posts that start with "I don't feel inspired to write tonight, but I made a commitment to write something every week, so here I sit with the clock ticking away the minutes." Ugh.

> "Your first draft is what you need to say; your final draft is what your reader needs to hear.

We may need to begin our draft like that because it helps us gain some traction and discover our meaning. These kinds of introductions may provide the scaffolding we need to get the writing done. I'm all for it. But the reader does not need it. Cut that stuff out.

Cut the Ending

I've just finished reading a popular novel. I adored the book, except for one glaring problem—it is three chapters too long. Rather than concluding the book with a telling scene and a strong evocative ending, the author went on and on and on (and on) and summarized thirty-plus years in the life of this family. This clumsy, bloated, superficial ending spoiled the whole book for me.

Whether in fiction or nonfiction, poetry, songwriting, or blogs, sometimes less is more. As you revise your work, look for places where you over-explain, include too many details, or take it too far. Be especially concerned when you notice yourself re-stating and summarizing. Trust your reader.

"Kill Your Darlings."

If you have heard any of the advice that Stephen King offers in his book *On Writing*, it is probably this three-word mantra: Kill your darlings. King is emphatic: "Kill your darlings, kill your darlings, even when it breaks your egocentric little scribbler's heart, kill your darlings." It is brutally difficult to delete any part of your story, any event in your memoir, any stanza in your poem, or any scene in your play. It hurts. We cut the text, and it feels like we bleed.

Here's the bad news. In fact, here is the worst news that I will give you in this whole book: Often, the secret to making your work better is cutting out your favorite parts. The really well-written parts. The parts that are beautifully expressed. The parts that convey deep emotion, offer brilliant insight, or are written in the most gorgeous prose.

But why in the world would you ever cut the best stuff?

Because when you revise, you are not trying to cut the bad stuff and keep the good stuff. Listen. When you revise, you must be determined to *keep only the stuff that belongs*. The stuff that relates directly to your central message. The dialogue that advances the plot. The scenes that move the action forward. The rest of it? Kill your darlings. Do it.

Save the Scraps

When I encourage writers to delete anything that isn't doing any work, I get resistance. If I can convince them that this step is tried and true, they challenge me with a practical question. What does "delete" mean? I mean, should I literally hit the "delete" key?

Sometimes. Sometimes a sentence, scene, or section has served its purpose. More often, though, writers find it useful to save the scraps. You never know how a stray sentence, paragraph, description, dialogue, or stanza will be useful down the line:

- To use as a blog post or material for a newsletter.
- To turn into a double-nickel story (exactly fifty-five words).
- To shape into a poem.
- To offer as bonus material for readers and supporters.
- To enrich a different term paper, review, or essay.
- To post on social media.
- To serve as the starting place for a sequel or for a different project altogether.
- To shape into a presentation or work into an interview.

As I revise a work, I often cut material and then move it to the end of the document. There, I draw a line and label the section "STRAY BITS." I change all the text in that section to blue. If I decide that I need that sentence, paragraph, story, or list, it's easy to find it, copy it, and move it back.

When I've finished the work, I collect the spare bits and move them to a separate document. I have a folder on my computer's desktop for "Deleted Bits." Some people organize their scraps by topic or project to make them easier to find later. When I need material for a talk or a Facebook post, I'll scroll through and see if any of this old material is the right starting point for this new purpose. Often, these raw materials take on new life when considered in a brand-new context.

Consider this advice from C. S. Lewis. He writes, "When you give up a bit of work, don't (unless it is hopelessly bad) throw it away. Put it in a drawer. It may come in useful later. Much of my best work, or what I think my best, is the rewriting of things begun and abandoned years earlier." Save those scraps, experiments, false starts, and dead ends. They may pave the way for something fresh and new.

So pull out the chainsaw. Cut away. The work you have done is not lost, even if it doesn't appear as part of this project. It may not find new life in another project, either. But it will show up in the difference it makes *in you.* No matter what happens to the material we have drafted, we are being shaped and changed. We are becoming better writers.

ADD IT
Learn to Elaborate

Revising includes finding the best order for the material and then clearing away the deadwood. What's next? It's time to see what to add. I often work with students who are frantic because their paper is only two pages, and it's supposed to be five. "I've already said everything I can think of. I have made every point I have to make. I have nothing else to say." And then they add, "Besides, I'm a concise writer."

Maybe. Let's say that a student has been asked to write an essay about the characteristics that identify Odysseus as an epic hero in *The Odyssey.* They write an essay that looks something like this:

> Odysseus isn't a big, brawny guy who gets all famous by flexing his muscles. What really makes him heroic is that he is smart. He figures out the whole Trojan horse idea. He figures out a clever way to listen to the song of the sirens. When he blinds the Cyclops, he makes sure he has a plan in place so he doesn't get trapped forever in that cave. When he gets home, he arrives in disguise so he doesn't get murdered by those suitors. He's smart and strategic. That's what makes him a truly epic hero.

Not a bad start. First, they have identified an important tension or conflict that shapes the essay and adds interest. Although we usually view heroes in terms of their physical abilities, Odysseus is considered a hero because of his intellectual prowess.

But what could I say to this writer who has already listed every single reason he can think of to prove her point? Look at the essay again: The student has identified four main situations that demonstrate the way Odysseus uses his intellect. However, the student has not developed or described any of them. Rather than searching around for more examples, she needs to go back and develop the claims she has already made.

Take the Trojan horse event, for example. Rather than merely mentioning it, this student should describe the scene. Develop details by explaining why it is such a smart solution. What specific problems does it solve? In what way is it innovative? Then add details to amplify the point. Are there any quotations in the text that support the wisdom of Odysseus' course of action? Are there any observations from scholarly articles that shed light on this important scene? Are there any quotations from class lectures or insights from fellow students that were made during class discussions that can help to back up this assertion?

If she wants to go even deeper as she elaborates on the importance of the Trojan horse event, there are other ways to expand and support this example. Compare it to other wise actions by other heroic figures in other stories. Bring it into focus by contrasting it with another scene or a different hero in *The Odyssey*. Refine the definition of "heroic" and show its broader meanings. Offer a hypothetical example. How do you add support and expand your text? By adding details, describing scenes, elaborating reasons, explaining concepts, and supporting claims.

A piece of writing is transformed from a bald sequence of statements to a rich conversation when we take time to develop our ideas.

This is the magic of adding. It doesn't just apply to student essays, and it's not just about supporting a claim. As they revise, writers have a whole host of options they can use to make their writing richer and more well-rounded. A fiction writer might provide more information about a character's history or do more to flesh out an important setting, bringing it to life in the reader's mind. A blogger might add quotations from an article to shore up their credibility. A self-help book might describe a case study or follow a hypothetical character through the steps of a process.

Here are a few of the most common opportunities for meaningful addition.

Add Material for Consistency

Just as you may notice some parts of the text are way too long, you may also notice thin patches in the manuscript. Do you have a story in every chapter except for Chapter 4? Are all your chapters around two thousand words—except for one that's only five hundred? Is one of your characters the only one without a backstory?

These are all examples of where a writer should consider adding text. The goal here is not to enforce strict uniformity but to create *rhythm*. Rhythm is made up of patterns. Consistent choices in length, tone, and content allow our readers to relax. Consistency offers them a general sense of where you are leading them—like knowing that each chapter in this book will include a magic trick and end with a summary. You know what to expect. If one of these elements were missing, your attention would automatically be drawn to it.

Breaks in the pattern can be confusing or frustrating, and, above all, distracting. Adding for consistency gives your reader a sense of security and keeps their focus on your message.

Fill Intuitive Gaps

The unfortunate reality is that much of what we *think* we said has not actually made it to the page. But the reader is reading your text, not your mind. After taking some space and looking at the writing in a new way, consider the following questions. Where have I made intuitive leaps? Where have I moved from point A to point C without including point B? Where have I left out the explicit links that show my reader how the parts connect? Where do I assume the reader knows something they might not know?

As the expert in your subject or the visionary of your story, these connections are obvious to you. Slowing down to flesh them out may seem tedious and unnecessary. It is not. This is the selfless work of writing for our audience, not for ourselves.

Support Your Claims

Writers can get stuck in the trap of making repeated claims or assertions without elaboration. When they do, they are asking readers to believe them "because I said so." The writing also comes across as vague and flat. Consider the following claims:

> Curtis was tired of working so many extra hours at his job.
> Clifford trained hard to prepare for the upcoming concert.
> Athletes must stay hydrated.
> Remodeling your kitchen is stressful.

These statements are fair and believable. But they are generalizations. They are simple claims, hard to picture, and, frankly, rather boring to read. What specific details, facts, and examples might be added to flesh out each of these ideas?

My students often try to develop their point (and increase their word count) by simply restating exactly the same claim in several different ways. Consider this frustrating, redundant paragraph:

> Remodeling your kitchen is stressful. If I had known how hard it was, I don't think I would have done it. It's honestly overwhelming. I'm tired all the time. I can't wait until this process is over. I am stretched to my limit.

Contrast that paragraph with this one that uses specific examples to make the point:

> Remodeling your kitchen is stressful. It completely disrupts your normal daily routine. Having workers underfoot makes it hard to concentrate. The dust and noise add to the disruption. But perhaps the thing that annoys me the most is figuring out how to prepare healthy meals three times a day with nothing more than a mini-fridge and a microwave. Trying to maintain a semblance of normal family life during the remodeling process has me stretched to my limit.

Reflect on your work-in-progress. Identify the key sections, perhaps listing them on a separate sheet of paper or by highlighting them. Then evaluate the ways you are describing, describing, supporting, elaborating, and developing each assertion. Is your discussion limited? Is your argument thin? Add a story, an illustration, or an example. Put in a quotation. Develop a comparison or a contrast. Find ways to express emotion or appeal to the sense of hearing, touch, taste, or smell. Or perhaps offer a definition to clarify and elaborate your point.

Let It Go

Having worked hard to convince you that radical revision is an important key to becoming a happy and productive writer, I need to add a word about the dark side of revising. It can become an endless process of moving, deleting, and adding new material. I am not talking about productive revision, where every draft takes you just a little bit closer to the true meaning of the work. After all, Ernest Hemingway, a famously concise writer, said, "I rewrote the ending to *A Farewell to Arms*, the last page of it, thirty-nine times before I was satisfied."

Rewriting is crucial. But revision can become a black hole that writers fall into and never escape. It's so hard to resist tinkering with this sentence and then with that one, making connections and discovering new meanings. Donald M. Murray writes, "We could go on, revising this draft for a week, a month, a year, and some writers—or nonwriters—have gone on writing for a lifetime."

The cycle is driven by the conviction that this draft can always be made better. It's true; it can. I get it. I assumed my first book was my magnum opus, and it took me twenty-three years to write. I can hardly stand to look at it now because I am painfully aware of errors that slipped by and limitations that I did not recognize at the time.

Your legacy may be one perfect poem or one peerless novel, but perhaps, for now, good enough is good enough. At some point, you have to unclench your fists and let it go, warts and all. Remember, an imperfect book can make a mighty difference in someone's life. An unwritten one cannot. Besides, you've got other projects and other priorities. Take a deep breath and move on.

Chapter 8 Summary
REWORK

- The first step to making good writing better is not to polish it, but to radically re-envision what it can be.
- Take a step back and try reading in a different format—different font, different size, or a printed page instead of the screen—to gain a fresh perspective.
- Review the structure, and consider preparing a reverse
- outline to get a sense of the big picture and find the best order.
- Ask: Is there anything in the text that does not advance my story or contribute directly to my meaning?
- Be bold about removing what doesn't belong, but save it as scraps to use as raw material for new projects.
- Check the proportions so they reflect the emphasis you want to communicate.
- Look for opportunities to add explanations, illustrations, and examples to support your point and enrich your content.

The Big Idea

Before you start fiddling with editorial details, refine your content and strengthen your structure.

Take a Step

Look at a draft, either an old project or something you are currently working on and see if you can add strength and clarity by deleting unnecessary material.

A Final Word

Revising requires sustained effort to step back from the details and gain a clear picture of the work as a whole. That is the reason most writers are tempted to skip it. Don't! Take the time needed to review sequence and proportion, clarify your focus, cut extraneous material, and add vibrant detail. Doing so will vastly improve everything you write.

Chapter 9
EDIT
Refine Your Style

In Chapter 8, we looked at revising. We focused our attention on strengthening our content and reviewing the structure. The next step in the writer's process is *editing*. We revisit our draft, shifting our focus away from *what* we are saying and paying close attention to *how* we are saying it. Here again, the priority is anticipating the reader's needs. However, while revision focuses on the forest, editing focuses on the trees—specifically, individual sentences and word choice.

What is editing? Many people use the word as an umbrella term to describe any attempt to refine their writing. The red pen comes to mind. But that's not how I am using the term in the Pathway Approach. I'm not using it to describe either the big-picture work of revision or the minutiae of proofreading that comes next.

Editing is making improvements at the sentence level to make your expression more effective. It addresses these key questions. How can I be clearer? More compelling? How can my sentence length and sentence structure support my meaning? How can my word choice help me connect to my reader?

Some writers call this "style." My students call it "flow."

Here is another way to think about the work of editing. This is the time to give your full attention to the way the text sounds and the impression it makes. We add finesse. We adjust sentences to achieve variety and emphasis. We refine word choice to attain the greatest possible accuracy and eloquence. We consider qualities such as voice and tone. Is it too formal for this audience? Or too casual? Is it cold and distant? Too commanding? Just plain chatty? Is it bland, functional, flat, and mechanical? Or does it sound like a real person who has something important to say?

Why is editing so important? Because the best writing is immersive. When our writing is strong, our readers get caught up in the story, the argument, the description, or the discussion. Ideally, they completely forget that they are reading. They are carried along the stream of meaning, unhampered by poor stylistic choices such as awkward phrasing or irritating redundancies. They lose themselves in the prose.

Editing creates a seamless, satisfying reading experience. That is the goal when we give time and attention to editing. As Stephen King asserts, "To write is human, to edit is divine."

Here's what to look for when editing:

Appropriate: Does the way I've written this fit my ideal reader? Does my word choice carry the same connotations to my reader that it does to me? Will they think my words sound dated? Trendy? Obscure? Will my diction offend or exclude? Is it too formal or informal?

Compelling: Do my words and sentences underscore my meaning? Do I use short sentences for emphasis, and long, complex sentences to focus attention? Have I avoided overusing certain sentence patterns? Is there a pleasing variety and natural rhythm in the text? Is there clunky word choice, a lapse in tone, or an odd or quirky phrase that draws attention to itself and away from the reading experience?

Clear: Are too many words muddying my point? Are my sentences arranged so the progression of my ideas is easy to follow? Could a statement be misconstrued?

The mantra for editing is simple: *Say it better.* At this stage, we welcome the inner critic's help. We consider how even minor decisions, such as word order, can express our personality and communicate our meaning.

This book offers a big-picture overview of the writing process—a pathway from blank page to finished manuscript—so the treatment of editing will be brief. This chapter will suggest just a few of the most important elements that help authors improve the impact of their prose.

Appropriate: Does It Fit Your Reader?

Again, for this next stage, we are not asking "Is the writing good?" Or even "Is the writing correct?" We are asking, "Is this appropriate for my reader?" This question has informed your drafting and revising. In editing, this same question continues to guide the many decisions that shape a writer's style.

These decisions may seem minor, but their consequences can be enormous. Consider the work of Audrey, an author from Abigail's coaching practice. Audrey is a "plain language expert" who specializes in health literacy. In other words, she helps everyday people understand what their doctor or healthcare system is actually telling them amid all that confusing medical jargon.

During one consultation, Audrey read through a handout that her client had received from a local clinic. This was the first sentence she saw: "The half-life of this medication necessitates bi-daily administration to maintain therapeutic plasma concentrations."

She closed her eyes for a second and shook her head. The language sounded as if it were written for a pharmacist or doctor. And for those specialists, the sentence would have been perfect. But who was it intended for? The scared, middle-aged woman sitting across the table from her, who had just been diagnosed and was trying to remember how to take her new medication.

Audrey picked up a pen and rewrote the sentence: "Take one pill in the morning and one at night. This keeps a steady amount of medicine in your body."

Health literacy studies show that people forget 50% of what the doctor says before they even walk out the door. The average medical form is written at a college or high school reading level; the average U.S. adult reading level is grade eight. Can you imagine the consequences of people not understanding how to take their medication, when to schedule a check-up, or how to see a specialist? All because of word choice. Sentence length. Form and formality.

Communication is not always a matter of life and death, or health and wellbeing, but Audrey's work illustrates an important principle: Adapting to our audience can make a world of difference, determining whether your message goes in one ear and out the other or has a truly transformational impact on your reader's life.

With that in mind, let's explore a few key ways to say it better for our reader.

Think About Form and Genre

A text message with too much punctuation might come across as hostile. An email to a potential employer filled with "lols" and "I dunnos" might cost someone a job. An academic book with too many sentence fragments might give the reader doubts about the author's credibility. A memoir with too formal a tone could undermine the essential writer-reader connection. A form for the insurance company must be written a particular way, but I am not an insurance form, and I would not want my doctor to speak to me as if I were.

When you edit, you're not just fixing sentences. You're asking whether the writing fits the form it's meant to take. Form includes the physical medium—text message, email, book—as well as the genre you're working in.

We make many of these adjustments instinctively—we use one form to message a friend, another to email our boss. Others may require more thought. Journalistic paragraphs tend to be short; academic ones are often longer. School essays and speeches usually have introductions and conclusions; friendly letters do not. Different genres of fiction follow different conventions. Poetry delights with visual signals and creative wordplay.

Each type of writing operates by a logic of its own.

Enter Your Reader's Context

Consider the differences in the following two sentences.

> Most of the L. A. River looks like a giant concrete ditch, but in some stretches it's still a real, living river—with water, plants, birds, frogs, and pockets of wetlands—and more of it is slowly being restored.

> While much of the L. A. River is channelized, several reaches retain or have regained naturalized conditions that support riparian habitat, avian species, amphibians, and emergent wetland ecosystems, with ongoing restoration expanding these areas.

Who do you think the first one was written for? The second?

The first example is informative but casual, requiring no prior expertise on the subject to understand. The second one expresses the same idea, but it's written for someone who likely already has some background in ecology.

To an expert, the first version comes across as insulting—it doesn't acknowledge what they already know. To a layperson, the second sentence is so dense that they might miss the point entirely.

We must adapt our writing to the reader and our relationship with them, also known as "rhetorical stance." But notice how I didn't lead with "We must edit for our rhetorical stance" because while you may know that term, I'm not assuming most of our readers have a background in English, composition, or communications.

Continuing with our medical example, what if the patient were an eight-year-old? The doctor would be wise to find a way to explain the procedure in the language of mermaids and *Bluey*. Otherwise, that child would be afraid, confused, and uncooperative.

As you edit, consider your reader's prior knowledge, their age, culture, values, and priorities. Adjust your wording, sentences, and formality to match.

Consider the Level of Formality

On Saturday, I wore blue jeans, a flannel shirt, and boots to go hiking. On Monday, I'll dress for work in black pants, an olive-green blouse, and heels. Each of those outfits is mine; that is, each one reflects the colors and fabrics I like to wear and the idiosyncratic way I like to put outfits together. And each outfit is perfectly suited to the unique demands of the day.

That is true of writing as well. Each piece of writing should be suited to its unique context while at the same time reflecting what is unique about you. If you show up in the wrong outfit, you can still make it work. But how much more successful will you be if your clothing—and your prose—is perfectly suited to the situation?

Want to be a better writer? Expand your linguistic wardrobe. Explore new styles. Experiment with new possibilities. From casual working-in-the-garden storytelling to business casual emails to distinguished black-tie prose. Seek to have an all-occasion wardrobe of words at the ready. Informal. Formal. And every style in between.

When it comes to editing, dig deep into the more important question: Does this word, this sentence, and this paragraph do the important work it is supposed to do in this specific context? Is it appropriate here?

Compelling: Does It Engage Your Reader?

Once you've ensured your writing fits the situation—in form, context, level of formality, and so on—the next question is a different one. Does it *engage* the reader? Appropriate writing does its job, but compelling writing does more than that. It invites the reader in, holds their attention, and makes them want to keep reading. Here are a couple of ways to tailor your writing not just for suitability but for impact.

Curate Your Words

English is a remarkably flexible and powerful language, and it offers innumerable ways to say the same thing. As we've seen, you might edit your wording to suit your intended reader. But you also might edit your wording because there's a more accurate, beautiful, funny, or satisfying way to say what you mean.

> **Example:** "The movie upset her." (Acceptable but vague, as "upset" can imply sadness or anger.)
> **Stronger version:** "The movie enraged her." (More concrete and evocative.)

> **Example:** "She struggled to control her fear." (Totally fine, but could be stronger.)
> **Stronger version:** "Her fear strained at the leash." (Expresses the same idea but in a more creative way.)

> **Example:** "By the end of the day, I was tired." (Correct but colorless.)
> **Stronger version:** "By the end of the day, I was running purely on caffeine and poor decisions." (Adds color with mild humor and exaggeration.)

> **Example:** "He had poor posture." (A visual detail, but not particularly vivid.)

Stronger version: "His posture made him look like a question mark." (Conjures an immediate mental image.)

Strong word choice doesn't mean invoking four-syllable SAT words; it means choosing words that are more precise, concrete—words that help reinforce your tone and keep your reader engaged in not just what you're saying but how you say it.

Style Your Sentences

Word choices communicate style; how you string them together does as well. Consider the following example. In each of these sentences, you have a choice as a writer. Look at these three options:

Barbara had a cupcake; Rhonda ate a cookie instead.
Barbara had a cupcake. Rhonda ate a cookie instead.
Barbara had a cupcake, but Rhonda ate a cookie instead.

Three different sentences that say exactly the same thing. Or do they? Each of these three options is perfectly correct from a grammar teacher's point of view. But each is a little different in its emphasis.

The *first* one uses a semicolon. It looks a bit more official. And since it is a single sentence, it suggests that the two actions are somehow related to each other.

The *second* one, on the other hand, separates the two actions into two short, simple, declarative sentences. That sounds more informal. It looks more conversational. It's casual.

The *third* one uses a different connector—the word "but." This draws our attention to the idea of contrast. Instead of simply making two casual observations about who ate what, this construction emphasizes the way that Rhonda's choice stands in opposition to the choice that Barbara made.

Careful attention to sentence patterns in the editing process can help in a few really important ways. First, the way something is said can either underscore our meaning or subvert it. Long, elaborate sentences have the power to make one kind of impact on our readers; short ones make another. Word order can build slowly to a crescendo or hit the ground running right out of the gate.

Think about the differences in how a reader might experience these similar statements:

- Yongwon picked up some groceries and filled his car with a full tank of gas before embarking on the long drive to Nashville.
- Yongwon bought gas and groceries, then drove to Nashville.
- Before he left for Nashville, Yongwon took the time to purchase a few groceries and put some gas in the car.
- After buying groceries and then filling his car with a full tank of gas, Yongwon left for Nashville.

Changing the order of words changes the emphasis. Notice that in sentences 1, 2, and 4, "Nashville" is the final word, and so the location seems more important. But in sentence 3, when the location is buried in the middle of the sentence, the destination feels like an insignificant detail. Sentence structure helps writers place emphasis where it belongs.

Second, changing the sentence pattern also modifies the tone. Is Yongwon eager to leave, or is he delaying his departure? Sentence 1 makes the trip sound like a long excursion. Sentence 2 makes it sound like a run-of-the-mill stop. Sentence 3 makes Yongwon sound thoughtful and methodical. Sentence 4 makes it sound like he may have been using his errands as a way to postpone his departure.

Third, the structure of our sentences adds up line by line to create the music of our prose. All writers tend to fall into repetitive patterns: short, declarative sentences, or sentences with compound verbs, or sentences that use colons. None of these is problematic. The problem comes in when there is little variation from paragraph to paragraph. It gets sing-songy or dull. It numbs the readers rather than engaging them.

Gary Provost has been quoted far and wide for this brilliant illustration:

> This sentence has five words. Here are five more words. Five-word sentences are fine. But several together become monotonous. Listen to what is happening. The writing is getting boring. The sound of it drones. It's like a stuck record. The ear demands some variety.
>
> Now listen. I vary the sentence length, and I create music. Music. The writing sings. It has a pleasant rhythm, a lilt, a harmony. I use short sentences. And I use sentences of medium length. And sometimes, when I am certain the reader is rested, I will engage him with a sentence of considerable length, a sentence that burns with energy and builds with all the impetus of a crescendo, the roll of the drums, the crash of the cymbals—sounds that say listen to this, it is important.
>
> So write with a combination of short, medium, and long sentences. Create a sound that pleases the reader's ear. Don't write words. Write music.

Magic happens when we edit our work at the sentence level. Since you are no longer trying to figure out what to say, you can give your full attention to saying it in the most compelling way possible.

A final note on sentence structure. I often get asked if sentence fragments are okay. That is, can I use phrases that are missing a subject, verb, or complete thought? To answer that, you must first go back to consider your genre. For formal writing, it's not a fit. But in a short story? A blog? A novel or poem or memoir? Go for it.

Consider how the following fragments might add emphasis, rhythm, or intrigue: "Because I said so." "Until now." "Without a second thought." "The woman's scarf." Fragments also mimic the rhythms of speech, creating a more cozy, conversational voice. Use them purposefully, but use them.

Use Your Voice

Put together, these small but mighty stylistic choices begin to create what we call "a writer's voice." As Abigail tells her authors, voice is personality on the page.

Have you ever finished a book and thought, "I'd read this writer's grocery lists?" It's not just that you love what they say, but you are swept up in how they say it. Sometimes, you close the book feeling as if you know them. They represented themselves in a way that was so vivid and authentic that you connect with them without ever meeting. In fact, they conveyed a sense of voice without ever actually hearing their voice at all. No vocal inflections, facial expressions, or body language. Just the accumulation of small choices on a page. That's the magic of voice.

Voice is personality on the page.

In *The Art of Memoir*, Mary Karr says this:

> It certainly helps if the stories are riveting, but a great voice renders the dullest event remarkable. The secret to any great voice is the writer's finding a tractor beam of inner truth to shine the way. While an artist consciously constructs a voice, she chooses its elements because they're natural expressions of character .... Whatever people like about you in the world will manifest itself on the page. What drives them crazy will keep you humble. You'll need both sides of yourself—the beautiful and the beastly—to keep their attention.

"A tractor beam of inner truth." "Drives them crazy." "The beautiful and the beastly." Mary's own voice—in some ways plain and in some ways elegant—shines through her own quote.

How would you describe Anne Lamott's voice in the following quote from *Bird by Bird*?

> So now I teach. This just sort of happened. Someone offered me a gig teaching a writing workshop about ten years ago, and I've been teaching writing classes ever since. But you can't teach writing, people tell me. And I say, "Who the hell are you, God's dean of admission?"

Snarky yet warm, hyperbolic, and humorous. Those are words that come to mind. And I love her for it.

Think of these authors' unique voices:

- Hemingway: economical, straight to the point
- Toni Morrison: florid, vivid, sensory
- Malcolm Gladwell: informative, authoritative, clear
- John Green: smart, snarky, humorous
- Stephen King: blunt, dramatic, suspenseful
- Jane Austen: detailed, emotional
- Ocean Vuong: carnal, brief
- James Baldwin: rhythmic, elegant, witty
- Fyodor Dostoevsky: introspective, dark, moralistic

Genre informs voice to a degree. A self-help book might sound motivational through short, clear sentences. A philosopher's work abstract, complex, and subtle. A political writer's opinion piece could be analytical, authoritative, and earnest. A blogger expresses outrage. They use short sentences. Or even fragments.

When it comes to fiction, writers often create a sense of voice through tongue-in-cheek humor, ornate descriptions, or eccentric characters. Then they take it a step further. They work to ensure that each character is given a voice of their own.

Ideally, the reader will know who is speaking even without a dialogue tag. You know that line of dialogue is from one character because that character is a cynical, temperamental homebody, while the other is a whimsical, optimistic adventurer. Their lines of dialogue will be very different, and the reader will follow easily when the characters' unique voices have been developed. While the advice in this chapter is oriented toward helping you recognize and develop your writer's voice, you may find that these ideas help you to build convincing characters as well.

Fiction or nonfiction, blog or book, ask yourself, "How will I express my own sense of self on the page?" A writer's voice will shift across different genres and yet stay authentic to their nature. Here are some of the tools at your disposal:

- word choice
- italics
- capitals
- bold font
- punctuation
- sentence length
- repetition
- humor
- dialect
- fragments
- overstatement
- figurative language

Elements like these work together to help your reader feel like they're sitting in the room with you, like you are a real person interacting over afternoon coffee or sharing stories late into the night.

MAGIC TRICK
Reading Aloud

We've explored some ways to ensure the writing is both appropriate and compelling. As you do this, you may encounter one bit of advice for writers that crops up everywhere. It is this: If you want to hear the rhythms of your text, read it out loud. C. S. Lewis insists, "Always write (and read) with the ear, not with the eye." Lewis has the right idea. When your readers are working their way through your blog post, term paper, or novel, they hear the words in their head, reproducing the rhythms of your sentences and the texture of your word choice. Writing for the ear is important. Lewis tells us that you should "hear every sentence you write as if it was being read aloud or spoken. If it does not sound nice, try again."

However, the problem with trying to diagnose your own prose by reading it out loud is that you will read what you meant rather than what you said.

I have tested this hundreds of times with writers. For example, let's say that the following sentence appears in their research paper: "Odysseus needed to keep the goal in mind and prioritizes the welfare of his team rather the impulse of his appetites." If I ask the student to read that sentence out loud to me, two things are inevitable.

First, they will emphasize the words they think are most important: "Odysseus *needed* to *keep* the goal in mind and *prioritize* the welfare of his *team* rather than the *impulse* of his *appetites*." However, a casual reader may or may not read the sentence that way. Writers know what they mean, and, therefore, they pronounce things with a particular emphasis. But a reader does not know what the writer *meant*. They only have access to what the writer *said*.

Here is the second problem. When writers read their text aloud, they will almost always add missing words, word endings, or grammatical refinements. Look at the original sentence again. The word "prioritizes" should be "prioritize," and the word "than" is missing after the word "rather." As a reader, you may have noticed these two errors; on the other hand, you may have simply supplied them as you read. When writers read their sentences out loud, they're still likely to miss many of the errors they need to correct.

If C. S. Lewis and countless other writers are right, and writing "with the ear" is an essential component to better writing, then how can we get help with this? How can we get a sense of what the text sounds like in the mind of a reader?

If you are serious about strengthening the vigor and clarity of your work, there is one surefire way to do it: Have someone else read your text out loud to you. You gain insight into your work when you listen carefully to how your text sounds in the mind of your reader. The benefit is enormous. The effect? Pure magic.

There are many ways to practice this. If you are a student, ask a peer to read parts of your essay out loud. If you're a blogger, get a friend to read your upcoming post to you. If you're an author or other professional writer, ask a friend or editor to read you a chapter or a scene. Now, you probably won't find someone eager to read your three-hundred-page novel out loud to you. But having someone read even a page or two of your writing to you will give you the power to recognize patterns you couldn't see before.

There are also multiple tools, both online and on your phone, that will read your text out loud. They may read the text with a different cadence than a human reader, and yet they can still be very useful for finding errors and hearing how your writing sounds. With this new insight, you can go looking for those patterns and correct them in other areas of the text.

Listening to your own writing while a compassionate, interested reader reads your work aloud is one of my favorite magic tricks.

Clear: Is It Accessible for Your Reader?

Good writing is appropriate. It is compelling. It is also clear. Clarity allows the reader to follow your thinking and get caught up in your prose without strain or confusion. Here are a few concrete ways to guide your reader and remove obstacles that might cause them to wander.

Tailor Transitions

Imagine you are hiking. You are on a clear trail, and you took a photo of the map. But when the trail starts to narrow, you wonder if you are really where you need to be. When you get to a crossroads, you can't quite tell which direction you're supposed to go next.

As you round a corner, you see a signpost. A small sign—noticeable but not obtrusive—sticking out of the ground. It shows you where each of the converging paths leads and indicates your mile marker. You have been on the right path, and it's a relief to have it confirmed periodically as you travel.

This is the essential function of transitions—one of the most valuable ways to help a reader traverse your ideas with confidence. You are leading them on a journey, after all. A journey that builds and climbs and sometimes winds into unexpected yet purposeful territory.

Transitions happen on multiple levels. Here are some examples:

Between sections:
Part I of this book explored the L. A. River's transformation over the last century. In Part II, we'll explore its cultural and symbolic significance within the city.

Between chapters:
While the previous chapter focused on individual memory, this chapter examines how memory operates within communities.

Between paragraphs:
In addition to time and patience, baking bread also requires careful attention to temperature.

Between sentences:
He seemed nice enough. *On the other hand*, she had never gone on a blind date before.

The bathroom line stretched on for a mile. *As a result*, my marathon time was longer than expected.

The study draws on a wide range of sources. *That said*, it focuses primarily on urban populations.

Transitions are signposts that make it hard for your reader to get lost. They inform or remind the reader where they're located in the larger story. They let us know not only what you're introducing next but also why you're introducing it—how it builds on, contradicts, or adds greater nuance to whatever came before it.

A good transition does not simply state where we've been or where we're going next; it explains the relationship between ideas. Consider the following:

Weak transition: Many residents rely on public transit. This chapter discusses urban planning.

Strong transition: Many residents rely on public transit. As a result, transit planning directly affects their daily mobility and opportunities.

One of the best signposts to lead the reader through a progression of ideas is something you might remember from English classes: the topic sentence. The topic tells the reader what the paragraph is about and why it matters. Observe the topic sentence in the paragraph you are reading here. It introduced the idea of a topic sentence while framing it as part of our existing conversation, creating a clean transition and signaling what the rest of the paragraph would be about.

Transitions are signposts that make it hard for your reader to get lost.

Writers often bury the topic sentence late in the paragraph, so the signpost is obscured. Or string together multiple ideas in one mega-paragraph so the reader never has a transition to breathe. Or make a claim in the topic sentence, then repeat that claim throughout the paragraph, without adding new information.

As you edit, look for the hinges between sections, chapters, paragraphs, and sentences. Don't belabor the signposts, but offer your reader support and direction.

Scan for Repetition

In addition to weak or missing transitions, other factors challenge the reader along the way. Namely, clutter. Filler. Extra sentences, words, and phrases. These are like rocks in the path that distract readers. They are hazards that slow them down.

These obstacles are often a result of our effort to be understood. After all, they can't misinterpret me if I say my idea three different ways, right? Yet consider the following paragraph:

> The team struggled to move forward because it lacked clear leadership. Without someone to guide them, progress slowed to a crawl. The absence of direction made it difficult for the group to make decisions, and as a result, they found themselves stuck and unable to move ahead.

There's nothing incorrect about this paragraph. But notice how it simply repeats the same idea? Rather than stating your point, then explaining it and supporting it with reasons and examples, the three sentences say the same thing three times. Consider this revised sentence that makes the same point crystal clear in thirty fewer words:

> Without clear leadership, the team struggled to move forward. Decision-making stalled, and progress ground to a halt.

Now, don't go deleting all repetition. Repetition can play an important role in emphasis, reminding readers how concepts connect as they take in a lot of new information at once. Repetition can add depth, specificity, and emphasis.

Ask yourself if your repetition is serving a key function—to remind, recontextualize, connect, emphasize, or add nuance. But it must earn its place. If not, clear the clutter.

Look for "That"

The goal in editing for style is to make good writing better. And often, that means being more direct and concise. Sometimes the word "that" adds clarity, enhances your pacing, or underscores the tone you are creating. Otherwise? Let it go. Consider these examples:

> Jonas told me *that* he was hungry. → Jonas told me he was hungry.
> Rico thought *that* the game was on Tuesday → Rico thought the game was on Tuesday
> I believe *that* it will rain today → I believe it will rain today.
> We are so glad *that* you attended the lecture. → We are so glad you attended the lecture.

The book *that* I read was really good. → The book I read was good.

There are times, though, when the word "that" is exactly what you need to make your point:

That was a great halftime show.
I did not see *that* coming.
That gymnasium was haunted!

Using "that" is not an error. However, it is often unnecessary filler, and it can distract your reader. Use it wisely.

Avoid "-ly" Words

Words that end in "-ly" and modify a verb—these are adverbs, and they are seldom needed. Why? Because there is almost always a stronger verb that can take their place and allow you to streamline the sentence.

Generally speaking, avoid words that modify—*very* fast, *rather* timid, *pretty* cold, *sort of* complicated, *highly* competent, *extremely* dense, *basically* worn out, *actually* brand new. These slow your reader and water down the impact of your prose. The exception would be if you are intentionally creating a voice or a character that is meant to sound wordy, emphatic, or uncertain. In most other cases, though, Strunk and White refer to these qualifiers as "the leeches that infest the pond of prose, sucking the blood of words."

How do you address this? Replace adverbs with strong verbs. And keep an eye out for words that some people see as throwaways, such as really, constantly, generally, infrequently, extremely, awfully, relatively, slightly, actually, presumably, normally, and words like them. Search your document for -ly words, and see if your writing will feel more vibrant when you eliminate them.

Eliminate Compound Verbs

Another way to eliminate needless words and clear your reader's path is by weeding out compound verbs. A compound verb is when one thing does two actions at once.

This stylistic quirk is sometimes useful: She *mixed* the dough and *let* it rest. In this case, the verbs show the progression of moving from one action to another. But often, we end up with two verbs that serve the same function. Or one of the verbs is implicit in the other.

Wordy: She wiggled and fidgeted.
Streamlined: She fidgeted. (Fidgeting is a more specific form of wiggling.)

Wordy: You should learn to *refine and adjust* your sentence structures.
Streamlined: You should learn to *refine* your sentence structures. (Refine specifies that you should adjust in a way that makes the sentence better.)

Wordy: The committee met and discussed the proposal.
Streamlined: The committee discussed the proposal. (If they discussed, it's implied that they met to do so.)

Wordy: She sat down and rested on the chair.
Streamlined: She rested on the chair. (If she's in a chair, it's implied that she's sitting.)

As you edit, search for the word "and." When you see a compound verb, ask yourself if each verb is doing important work. If not, try to simplify the sentence. It may seem like a small difference, but attention to detail is a form of care for your reader, ensuring they have everything they need to complete the journey you've set before them, with nothing added to weigh them down.

A Word of Warning

When we think about our favorite authors and the books we return to again and again, we realize that it's not just the content, but the quality of the writing itself that enchants us. And it's not just something we admire in others; honestly, it's our hope when we think about the work we do.

That said, I want to issue a warning. Now that we've spent some time on elements of style—finding the right verb, minimizing adverbs, simplifying compound verbs—some writers are tempted to try to incorporate all of these suggestions and edit their text *as they write.* As I emphasized in Chapter 6, to make rapid progress during the drafting stage, we need to relax our grip, lower our standards, and focus on our message. It takes an enormous amount of energy to say what we mean. Once we have a handle on our message and key content, we can shift gears and attend to the details. Just get it down. *Then* turn your attention to getting it right.

To be clear, the more familiar you become with the power of a carefully chosen word or a beautifully structured sentence, the more you will naturally adjust the way you create a draft. However, it is madness to try to create text and evaluate text at the same time. It's like trying to knit a sweater while simultaneously unraveling it. It's like trying to play tennis while thinking about hand position, footwork, your opponent's actions, the visitors in the stands, and what you are having for lunch. It's a surefire formula for giving yourself a fatal case of writer's block.

So relax as you draft. Focus on the right content, the vivid example, the telling phrase. Something feels off or awkward? Mark it. Make it bold, color-code it, or add a quick bit of scaffolding, a "note to self" reminding you to revisit it. Refuse to get seduced down the dead-end path of trying to polish at the same time you are trying to produce the text in the first place. Give it your best shot, and press on.

Chapter 9 Summary
EDIT

- Work line by line and say it better.
- Choose words and sentence patterns to suit your reader.
- Strive to be compelling and clear.
- Let your unique voice shine through.
- Consider the sound of the text and not just the meaning.
- Add transitions as signposts.
- "Omit needless words."
- Don't try to draft and edit at the same time.

The Big Idea

Once you have enriched your content and fortified your structure, turn your attention to individual words and sentences and see if you can improve clarity, effectiveness, and grace.

Take a Step

Take a look at a few samples of your writing and see what you discover about your patterns of word choice and sentence structure. If possible, have a friend read a section out loud to you. What do you notice about the music of your prose?

A Final Word

The more time you devote to editing your work, taking time to review your work through the lens of word choice and sentence structure, the more you will find your instincts improving at the drafting stage. This step does more than help you create a better draft. This step strengthens your skills. You will become a better writer.

Chapter 10
PROOFREAD
Fix Mistakes

You've revised to ensure you've got the right information in the right order. You've edited so the writing is clear, cogent, and sounds authentically like you. Now, it is time for the final polish. It's time for proofreading.

What is proofreading? Proofreading is the final stage of re-writing, and it focuses on eliminating any remaining errors and double-checking the format and layout. Proofreading is the last line of defense against mistakes. This is the most detail-oriented part of the writing process and the final stretch before a piece of writing is completed.

Proofreading is largely about correctness. Here, the author ensures every comma is in its place and every typo is banished. This is also the stage to check whether your writing aligns with a style guide, such as Chicago, APA, or MLA, or conforms to a publisher's guidelines. Each one has unique rules on things like commas, capitalization, and how we credit our sources.

Beyond correctness, though, proofreading is also the last chance to check that even the most minor decisions on the page reflect your intent. Small errors can change your meaning. Omit needed punctuation, and you may end up saying something quite different from what you intended. Perhaps you have seen this warning in the form of a meme or a T-shirt: "I Like Cooking My Family and My Pets." Those missing commas change the meaning and thwart the writer's intent. This statement is usually accompanied by a warning: "Use commas. Don't be a psycho."

Statements like "Let's eat Grandma!" give us pause, but most punctuation errors are not fraught with imminent danger. Nevertheless, making time to attend to the details—comma usage, spelling, punctuation, grammar, formatting—invites your reader to focus their full attention on the substance of your story. Punctuation tells our readers what to emphasize, where to pause, and how our ideas are connected.

Here's how Russell Baker puts it:

> When speaking aloud, you punctuate constantly—with body language. Your listener hears commas, dashes, question marks, exclamation points, quotation marks as you shout, whisper, pause, wave your arms, roll your eyes, wrinkle your brow. In writing, punctuation plays the role of body language. It helps readers hear the way you want to be heard.

In short, thoughtful punctuation helps good writers communicate their meaning.

Proofreading also goes beyond just the words on the page. It includes taking a final look at citations, titles, subtitles, formatting, images, boxes, tables, page breaks, page numbering, and the Table of Contents. It means looking for consistency in format: headings, indents, and spacing. If the writing is going to take a physical form, like a book, magazine, or printed paper, a proofreader's job is even more robust, checking both the digital and then also the printed version for any flaws.

You'd think that after multiple rounds of drafting, revising, and editing, few errors would remain. Unfortunately, plenty of errors hide in plain sight despite repeated scrutiny. For this reason, proofreading does not just happen once but again and again, sometimes by several different people.

To some, this stage is satisfying and fun—after all, it's the final stretch. It is concrete and measurable, precise and methodical. And it is immensely satisfying to watch the text become clearer, cleaner, and stronger.

For others, this stage is irritating—reading the same page over and over, only to find something new to fix. I am in the second group. I do not enjoy proofreading.

Like it or not, here's the truth: Writing can be thorough, accurate, clear, and well-supported, but if it is riddled with small errors, the reader will be distracted. Think of a window pane, fly-specked and smudged with fingerprints. It draws attention to itself, making it harder to see the landscape unfolding behind it. Similarly, attention to accuracy removes obstacles and distractions. It clears the glass. It reveals the view. Correcting errors allows a writer's message to shine through.

As we have seen, the goal when revising is to be sure we have the right information in the right order. The goal when editing is to say it better: to make each sentence more appropriate, more compelling, and more clear. And the goal when proofreading is to find mistakes and fix them—and remove anything that distracts from your message.

The Key to Good Proofreading

Good proofreading requires that you try to ignore the content and see the words, phrases, and sentences for themselves. Remember those worksheets and grammar exercises from your school days? You ignored *what was being said* and focused exclusively on *how it was being expressed*—structure, form, pattern. Proofreading is a visual exercise.

The keyword here is *patience*. Work slowly and methodically. Work sentence by sentence in short blocks of time. Don't try to do it all at once or go too fast, or else you will skip over the details you need to fix. Patience. You're almost there.

Most people find it easier to proofread a printed copy rather than text on a computer screen. Pens, highlighters, and other analog tools can help as you hunt down errors and identify problems. Some editors recommend using a ruler to help you stay focused as you scan the text line by line.

If you do proofread on a screen, something as simple as making the font bigger can help you isolate individual words and sentences.

Like the editing chapter, this proofreading chapter is not intended as a comprehensive guide. However, understanding proofreading principles and fixing even a few of the most common mistakes can make a huge difference. I'll mention just a few key issues here.

MAGIC TRICK

Start at the End

When we process information, the brain does not take in information the way a computer does. Instead, we combine what we see with assumptions about what we expect to see given what we know from experience. That's why we can read words when they're misspelled. We know "wrting" is meant to be "writing." We skip the details to focus on higher-level tasks, such as understanding the meaning of what we read.

This is precisely why it is so challenging to proofread our own work. We wrote the material, so we know what we are trying to say. Our brain, trying to be helpful, fills in the gaps and skips over our mistakes. This is a major problem when those details are exactly what we're trying to find and repair.

For that reason, there are ways to trick ourselves and see our writing with fewer assumptions. One strategy is to read our writing from end to beginning rather than beginning to end. Start on the last page of your manuscript or the last word of your email. Read from the end to the beginning, sentence by sentence. Because you don't quite know what's coming next, you are forced to exert more energy and notice what's actually on the page.

Is this tedious? It can be. You'll need to go slowly and allow enough time. But the sudden ability to see what you missed is almost magic. It can be a lifesaver, too, especially if catching these types of details doesn't come naturally to you.

Different Contexts, Different Rules

Throughout this book, I've described this concept: Rather than asking "What's *correct*?" we need to ask, "What's *appropriate* for this context?" What's acceptable for a social media post may not be acceptable for a book. What's correct in a journalism class may be problematic when writing in a literature class. This applies to proofreading, too. Often, we will see something labeled "incorrect" when it is, in fact, completely correct—in a different context. Consider the following examples.

Is it Academic or Non-Academic?

It is not surprising to learn that our word choice is more elevated and our sentence structure more complex in an academic setting. What is surprising is that, depending on the circumstances, the particulars of grammar change, too.

One difference concerns the Oxford comma. In a list of three or more items, the Oxford comma is the final comma that is used right before the conjunction, that is right before words like "and," "or," "but." It is sometimes called a "serial comma" or a "series comma." It looks like this: "lions, tigers, and bears." Here are more examples:

> **With the Oxford comma:** Sierra grabbed her lunch, a dictionary, and a bouquet of flowers.
> **Without the Oxford comma:** Sierra grabbed her lunch, a dictionary and a bouquet of flowers.

With the Oxford comma: My dog barks at skateboards, other dogs, and anyone wearing a hat.
Without the Oxford comma: My dog barks at skateboards, other dogs and anyone wearing a hat.

With the Oxford comma: Can you pick up some Thai food, sushi, or fried chicken?
Without the Oxford comma: Can you pick up some Thai food, sushi or fried chicken?

The Oxford comma causes heated arguments—feelings on this run deep. My friend David has a coffee mug declaring his allegiance to the Oxford comma. It identifies him as a member of "The Oxford Comma Preservation Society." And I confess, I have a T-shirt that says, "Peace, Love, and the Oxford Comma."

What's the rule? It depends.

The Oxford comma is required in school, whether in second grade or graduate studies, as well as in more formal writing such as scholarly books and articles. Those who favor it say it is more precise and less likely to cause confusion.

On the other hand, the Oxford comma is omitted in journalistic writing and other less formal settings. Some consider it pretentious and believe that omitting it makes the writing feel more friendly and personal. Others think it clutters up the text and interferes with the reader's experience. In ads and other visual media, the Oxford comma "takes up space," and it is left out for that reason.

A second difference between academic writing and non-academic writing concerns the guidelines for using contractions. A contraction is made by shortening and combining two words. For example, "I+have" becomes "I've," "can+not" becomes "can't," "you+would" becomes "you'd," and so on.

What's the rule? It depends. Contractions are correct, even welcome, in spoken discourse. In fact, there is something off-putting about a person who never uses them. Consider the difference between saying "I don't want to do that" and "I do not want to do that," or "I'm sorry, I can't help you right now" and "I am sorry, I cannot help you right now." The latter examples sound both stilted and tense. Contractions are also terrific for creating realistic dialogue in a novel. However, they are not appropriate for academic writing. Most schools prefer that you avoid contractions in classroom assignments.

Endless ink has been spilled over the use of the Oxford comma, contractions, and other grammatical preferences. Overall, the most important thing to remember is that sometimes "correctness" depends on the context of our writing. What genre? What country? What style guide? Some guidelines remain consistent while others will vary depending on the context.

Is it British or American?

The Irish writer George Bernard Shaw once said that England and America are "two countries divided by a common language." I probably wouldn't go that far, but it is amusing to discover that words like "boot," "bonnet," "pants," and "biscuit" have different meanings depending on where you are from.

We think of English as being one language, but there are many dialects and many versions around the world. We may read books written and published in English; however, we may not notice that books published in Great Britain follow British conventions rather than American ones. Many of my very best students grew up reading children's classics like *The Wind in the Willows*, *Alice's Adventures in Wonderland*, or *The Hobbit*. They were drawn to beloved series such as The Chronicles of Narnia, *The Borrowers*, or *The Railway Children*. Or the tales of Peter Rabbit, Squirrel Nutkin, Paddington Bear, and the Velveteen Rabbit. All British. Not to mention Winnie-the-Pooh and Doctor Doolittle.

These classics all follow British conventions. Therefore, many of my very best students are frustrated that the writing standards they grew up with are marked as mistakes on the papers they submit to me in class. When I point out to them that those beloved stories were published in Great Britain, many are greatly relieved to have an explanation, even if they now need to learn and practice the conventions of American writing.

Here are some of the most common differences in terms of spelling:

British/American
colour/color
fulfil/fulfill
skilful/skillful
defence/defense
programme/program
axe/ax
judgement/judgment
behaviour/behavior
honour/honor
centre/center
analyse/analyze
theatre/theater
aeroplane/airplane
cheque/check
cosy/cozy
grey/gray

Typically, neither variations in vocabulary nor these differences in spelling cause much concern for American students. It's viewed as a quirk rather than a problem. However, there is one significant difference between the British and American styles that causes constant problems—the placement of punctuation with quotation marks.

British: I love the poem "Jabberwocky". It is from *Through the Looking Glass*.

American: I love the poem "Jabberwocky." It is from *Through the Looking Glass*.

British: I fell in love with her when she said, "I grew up in Cleveland".
American: I fell in love with her when she said, "I grew up in Cleveland."

British: My daughter "cleaned her room", but it was littered with dirty laundry.
American: My daughter "cleaned her room," but it was littered with dirty laundry.

In American English, the period or comma belongs inside the quotation mark. Those who grew up reading books written and published in England have a tough time with this rule. Due to repeated patterning, their instincts will insist that they look better *outside* the quotation mark. Because this habit is coded so early and associated with such positive memories, it can be very hard to break.

Is it Contemporary or a Remnant from the Past?

When I talk about comma rules in class, I often have one or two students who are not just resistant; they are upset. Maybe they have been reading a book for class or looking through an old magazine. Maybe they are enjoying a classic novel or reading an older translation of the Bible. And they notice that, despite what I told them, the author is using punctuation or syntax in a way that is not standard.

Sometimes it can be explained by the difference between academic and popular writing. Or between British and American English. There is another factor that affects grammar and usage: the time when something was written. That's because grammar rules change over time, and they can change significantly. This is easiest to see with vocabulary. We need a constant infusion of new words to explain or express new technological developments and cultural references. For example, *frenemy, helicopter parent, air quotes, ginormous, d'oh, biohacking, open source, clickbait, GIF,* and *facepalm* are all relatively new terms that have been added to the dictionary.

Vocabulary changes—that makes sense. But so do other details of grammar and usage. History buffs will tell you that early American writers capitalized nouns to show importance or draw emphasis. They were influenced by continental languages such as German, which capitalizes nouns. When you read early documents such as "The Declaration of Independence," you see this trait in words like "Life," "Liberty," "Happiness," "Laws," "Nature," "Government," "Safety," "Free," "Rights," "Independent States," and even the word "People." By the 18th century, a movement toward standardization eliminated this usage.

Another example of a change over time is the use of the first person in academic writing. There was a time when writing for class or for a scholarly journal required that the writer judiciously avoid the use of *I, me, my,* or *mine*. Students were warned not only to avoid personal pronouns but also to avoid using personal experiences to explain concepts or illustrate principles in their essays.

In many cases, this has changed. Even the most demanding scholarly journals have come to accept the value of first-person writing.

One more example: The growing acceptance of the singular "they" in writing. Consider these sentences:

- The student opened their notebook and began to outline their paper.
- A new teacher is coming to our school. They just moved here from Nebraska.
- Find an author who can tell you about their experience with publishing.

Some will flinch. These sentences seem to break the rules of "agreement," that is, the number of the subject, singular or plural, is supposed to match up with the number of the pronoun, singular or plural. Some would prefer to recast these sentences with a strategy like this: "Find an author who can tell you about his or her experience with publishing." Or "Find authors who can tell you about their experiences with publishing."

Language changes, and often those changes reflect cultural shifts, rather than linguistic ones. While it was previously considered to be an error, the "singular they" is now endorsed by *The Chicago Manual of Style*.

What's the rule? It depends. What's the norm for your intended audience? Your specific context? Here, as elsewhere, you'll want to figure out what's most appropriate and least distracting given your circumstances, then proofread based on these expectations.

Keep Proofreading in Perspective

As a teacher and an editor, I need to distinguish between a writer who makes a host of different mistakes and one who makes the same error again and again. If a teacher or editor has marked every mistake, look again. It may be that you are not making many errors but struggling with one specific rule or tendency.

I have some personal experience with this. When I was writing my PhD. comprehensive exams, I referred to poet and critic T. S. Eliot more than a dozen times. The problem? In the fatigue and stress of the three days of doctoral exams, I couldn't remember how to spell his name. Therefore, at the absolute pinnacle of my scholarly life, I made repeated references to "T. S. Elliott." Yeah. I still sometimes picture that committee of professors reading my essay, giggling, and trying to figure out whether I deserved the PhD. after all.

While proofreading may seem daunting, you can typically resolve most errors with just a few fixes. Whether you are correcting your own writing or someone else's, look for the patterns. For me? If a word ends in -ence or -ance, I am likely to spell it wrong. I know I also struggle with words that are hyphenated. And I am notoriously bad with numbers.

If the very thought of proofreading makes you want to book a session at a rage room, digital tools can be a great help. We'll expand on the opportunities and cautions of these tools in the following chapter.

Whatever you're writing in whatever genre, keep track of your patterns and foibles. Make a list and keep it in mind during the proofreading stage. Just do the best you can in the time you have.

A Tolerance for Imperfection

I need to warn you about something that will make every perfectionist's skin crawl. No matter how much time and effort you spend reviewing your final manuscript, chances are you will not catch every single error. And yes, even most professionally published books by the most well-established and reputable publishers still contain errors. Of course, they shouldn't have many. But ultimately, books, essays, articles, etc.—anything produced by humans—is going to be imperfect.

There comes a time when we must admit that we've done all we can. If you find that error in your published book that made it past five people in eight rounds of copyediting and proofreading, pay it your respects. May we all seek to be as persistent.

Chapter 10 Summary
PROOFREAD

- Proofreading requires patient attention to details.
- Start at the end of the document and work sentence by sentence toward the beginning.
- Understand that spelling, punctuation, and grammar rules change depending on the circumstances.

The Big Idea

Errors in grammar and usage are not tragedies or sins. They are distractions that prevent readers from staying focused on the important things that you have to say.

Take a Step

Identify one or two common errors that have plagued your writing. Take a little time—one error at a time—to figure out what the rule is, how to implement it, and why it matters.

A Final Word

Grammatical errors are annoying and distracting, but they are not a measure of your talent as a writer or an indication of the value of your work.

PART FOUR
What's Next?

Start by doing what's necessary, then what's possible,
and suddenly you are doing the impossible.
attributed to St. Francis of Assisi

As I sit at my dining room table and draft this introduction, I'm thinking about the writers I have worked with in the past few months: a Master's student who just earned his degree, an undergraduate who submitted her first serious scholarly paper, a dear friend and writing buddy who is nearing the end of the first draft of her first book, a neighbor who has just gotten the courage to share a few of her poems, and a doctoral student who has submitted his dissertation and is waiting for his committee to schedule his defense. Each one started with an idea, analyzed the particulars of their project, gathered key content, reflected on the habits that help them to stay on task, and then applied themselves to drafting, revising, editing, and polishing their work. Each one has achieved something magnificent and, in many cases, something they didn't think they would ever be able to do.

Now, each one of these writers is asking questions about the next steps for their project: Turn the thesis into a book? Take those poems to an open mic night? Reach out to an editor, an agent, or a publisher?

And more. Each one is wondering, "What new projects are waiting, and how do I make space for them? What would it take to make writing a regular part of my life?"

In PART FOUR of *Write Like You Mean It,* I want to address some practical questions that may arise as you start strong, maintain momentum, and finally come to the end of a project's path. Chapter 11 describes the next steps if you are considering publication—why you might want to get outside help from an editor, and how you might evaluate some of the options that are available for getting your work into print. The final chapter, Chapter 12, outlines suggestions for making more room in your life so your creativity thrives.

What's next? Let's explore a bigger vision of your life as a writer.

Chapter 11 PUBLISH *Reach Your Readers*

Countless people dream about writing a book, and many begin the process. If you have persisted and completed your project, you have accomplished something remarkable. Once you have a finished manuscript, you may be wondering, "Now what?"

As writers ponder that question, many will think of publishing. It's thrilling to see your name in print, and humbling to hear that your words helped or inspired others.

However, I want to emphasize that while publishing is a great goal, it is by no means the only reason to write. Too many writers get stuck in the idea that all the work they put in will only mean something if they sell thousands of copies or get on the *New York Times* bestseller list. This is simply not true. There is a payoff for all the hard work, but it doesn't boil down to bestseller lists, sales numbers, or even publication itself.

The Benefit of Writing? It's Writing.

One of the greatest advantages of a completed manuscript is the fact that writing a book changes you. One of the authors that Abigail worked with wrote a self-help book that included powerful personal stories, many of which he'd completely forgotten about until he was prompted to reflect on his life and fill in the gaps. While stringing these events together, he was able to shape them into a larger narrative with fresh meaning, insight, and perspective. He developed deeper empathy and forgiveness toward his family.

Yes, he sold a lot of books, but he also gained a new sense of his own story, which was, in many ways, far more valuable.

When you have a completed manuscript, think about these important questions. How has the act of writing my story or this idea changed the way I understand it? What perspective have I gained in the process? How am I different now than I was when I started?

Other benefits of completing a manuscript include ways you've grown in your craft as a writer. Are you developing your style and finding your voice? Have you learned how to tell your own stories in a descriptive, engaging way that brings the reader into the scene and underscores the point you want to make? Did you radically restructure your manuscript and live to tell about it? Did you learn that you can go on field trips for research or muster the courage to conduct an interview?

The skills you have acquired may be more mundane. Maybe you learned how to use a colon or semi-colon, or you found a new writing software you like. Perhaps you learned that you don't always need to start writing at the beginning of your story—or that you proofread best when you start at the end of the manuscript. These are key writing skills, and they are incredibly valuable regardless of how well the book does on the market.

You may have also experienced broader changes that are difficult to put into words. Many writers develop greater insight into the creative process. Perhaps you learned to trust your creativity, let go of the need to be perfect, or let yourself play for the first time since childhood. What freedom we find in letting ourselves try new things and see what happens. Maybe the greatest takeaway is validating your identity as a writer—knowing for sure that this is your thing and you want to do more of it.

How has this accomplishment changed your character? Are you more disciplined, more resilient, or perhaps more diligent and determined? Have you cultivated a greater sense of what it takes to reach a major milestone? Do you have more patience and appreciation for the creative work of others?

Once you take this time to reflect on what a feat you've accomplished, there are many ways to achieve that sense of closure we crave. Whether you have any plans to publish or not, try printing out your manuscript. Even formatting and printing one copy can be satisfying. There is something about holding the printed pages in our hands that helps us process that we really did it.

We can also consider sharing our work. Not for critique, but for the sense of being heard, believed, known, and accepted by another person. Share it with one person or with a group you trust to hold your words tenderly and encourage you to keep going.

MAGIC TRICK

A Tiny Print Run

My daughter has four middle names. This has caused a surprising number of difficulties. For example, her birth certificate has an addendum. And her driver's license compresses two of her middle names and lists them as part of her first name. We think it is cool, but the inconveniences go on and on.

When Sierra was in fourth grade, one of the receptionists at her school was filling out paperwork for her, and each form she completed required different information and unique formatting. Frustrated, the receptionist looked at us and asked, "How did that baby get six names anyway?"

I really liked the way she worded the question: How *did* that baby get six names? It caught my attention and became the title of a book that Sierra and I wrote together. In it, we explained the beautiful, complicated way that she ended up with such a beautiful, complicated name.

We talked together about her story. I wrote very short sections of text. Sierra illustrated each page. I used her illustrations to design a simple cover.

Then I went online, found a company that printed books, and had them print some copies. In publishing, this is called a print run—only rather than printing thousands of copies, we printed five. When they arrived, they looked just like regular books, with bound pages and a glossy cover. Can you imagine the fun we had giving the receptionist at her elementary school a full-color, paperback copy? Magic.

The pleasure of collaborating on that book still makes me smile. We shared it with family and friends. A copy of it sits on my bookshelf, alongside the other books I've written. I will forever love this little book.

How about you? Is there a family story, a collection of poems, a powerful essay, a how-to manual, or another written work that you want to share? You could get a few copies printed and bound at an office supply store. Or you could take it a step further. You could hire someone to design a cover and format the interior, then reach out to any one of a host of companies that can print and bind one copy, ten copies, or fifty copies for you to purchase and distribute. This is great for legacy books, travelogues, memoirs, or a paperback collection of your family's favorite recipes. Or perhaps you want to create a special occasion book or hardcover edition to give as a gift to your family, friends, colleagues, or writing group. The quality of these short-run books is astonishing, the process is fairly simple, and the costs are minimal.

Should You Hire an Editor?

If you plan to publish, whether the print run will be large or small, you've likely wondered whether it's worthwhile to hire an editor. The creative process is a vulnerable space. Inviting someone else into that process—especially if you need to pay them—can be daunting.

When working with an editor, it's helpful to understand what an editor's role truly is. Many people misunderstand what editors do. When Abigail tells people she is an editor, many people immediately apologize for the grammar rules they don't know. Here's the truth: Good editors are not out to nitpick your flaws. Have you ever shared an idea you were passionate about with someone, and they got just as excited about it as you were? This is what a great editor is like—someone who catches the author's vision and uses their skill to help the author express it in the best way possible.

Can't I do it myself? To an extent. The problem is that everyone has blind spots. This is true not just of novice writers but of all writers. When we read our work, we know what we are trying to say. So it's nearly impossible for us to be objective. A trained outside perspective helps us catch what we're missing before we submit or publish, from typos to intuitive leaps to issues with genre, audience, or tone.

What an editor does depends on what type of editor they are. Here are the main types you'll find working as freelancers or on staff in publishing houses.

Book Coach

Not quite sure what your message is, or what the right form for your message might be? Still pondering the right genre, format, or audience? You might be looking for a book coach: someone to lead you through the writing process from the earliest stages. While they may offer developmental feedback, their primary role is to help you clarify your message and set a path to manuscript completion. They can help you analyze your task and optimize your workstyle.

Developmental Editor

A developmental editor focuses on the big picture of the work. They ask revision questions, helping you rework the content and structure: Is there a core message? Is the audience clear? Is the structure logical? Are the stories relatable? Are the characters believable? Are there any plot holes? This type of editor won't typically give you line edits but broader observations and recommendations that require reworking and rewriting. Some authors choose to hire a developmental editor early to guide them through the process.

Sensitivity Editor

Sensitivity editors are also concerned with content, but they read your manuscript with a particular goal in mind. They seek accuracy in portraying cultures, including religious affiliations, ethnic and racial groups, and specialty groups. You might find this kind of editor helpful if you are describing characters with special interests. Think of how irritating it is when you are watching a TV show and the characters fall into shallow stereotypes—football players, science fiction fans, college professors, or rock stars. Sensitivity editors can help you identify stereotypes and eliminate offensive language, sweeping generalizations, tokenism, misrepresentation, and clichés.

Line Editor

A line editor is someone who zooms in a layer closer than a developmental editor, focusing more judiciously on the actual text, helping you to say it better. Once the content and structure are in place, line editors help the writer say hone their sense of voice. They keep an eye on items like transitions, consistency, repetition, and tone. Overall, their job is to make the writing more engaging, elegant, and efficient.

Copyeditor

A copyeditor is someone who focuses on refining and clarifying the writing at the word and sentence level. Different from a line editor who focuses on style, a copyeditor's primary concern is mechanics. They focus on grammar, spelling, punctuation, capitalization, syntax, diction, verb tense, consistency, or tone. They may also help with fact-checking, citations, and bibliographies.

Typically, you send your work to a copy editor after you have finished revising. If you aim to work with a publisher, it is wise to consider hiring a copyeditor *before* you submit a manuscript to eliminate distracting errors and improve your chances of acceptance. If the publisher accepts your project, they generally provide the final copyediting.

Proofreader

A proofreader is someone who works through the final copy with a fine-toothed comb and eliminates any remaining errors. They often work with a fully formatted copy, catching any errors that occurred in design or layout. Beyond the text itself, they check other elements like page numbers, headings, indexing, layout, and, for a book or magazine, the two-page spread. Publishers often provide proofreaders and then return the formatted manuscript to the author for a final look.

Choosing an Editor

Whether or not you need an editor depends on your goal for your work. If you're planning to submit it for publication, it is wise to get help and direction from an editor. If you are hoping that your writing will support your business or reach an audience of thousands of readers, put your best foot forward by hiring an editor.

Planning to self-publish? You'll want to hire at least a copyeditor and a proofreader—or someone who does both. But I must say that a good developmental editor can easily become a self-publisher's best friend. They offer the big-picture feedback that can determine whether or not your book expresses the story you've invested so much time into telling. Beyond their notes, they can become a brainstorming partner, provide much-needed encouragement, and offer accountability. A developmental editor can easily make the difference between a book that achieves its purpose and one that sits untouched on Amazon. And if you are just beginning your project? A book coach is there to make sure you start strong.

What if you're not writing a book? An editor can be helpful even for smaller pieces of writing. Their feedback can show you patterns to look for when you self-edit. It might be too costly and cumbersome to hire an editor for every blog or social media post. But having someone review a few of these can help you create a self-editing checklist for the next ones you write.

There are some cautions to keep in mind when working with an editor. Most importantly, if you're hiring an editor yourself, make sure you hire the right type of editor for your needs. Don't assume they're all the same. You will be very disappointed if you're hoping for a quick proofread and instead receive the news that your main character is not believable or that an entire chapter is unnecessary.

Additionally, don't rush into working with an editor if you're not ready to receive critique. Sometimes your ideas are too fresh and your heart is too raw. Under these circumstances, even the most gentle feedback can be painful rather than instructive.

Finally, remember that the word "author" is related to the word "authority." Professional editors give recommendations, but the final say is always, always yours.

Other Ways to Get Help

In the months and years that have passed between the moment I sat in my home office and typed this sentence and the moment that you are now looking at this page and reading it, there are dozens, maybe hundreds, of new electronic programs, apps, and services that purport to assist writers with the nitty-gritty of grammar and style. Some are terrific. Some are worthless. And some do irreparable damage to your creativity by homogenizing your voice and weakening your instincts. Or compromise your integrity by inviting you to present something that you, in fact, did not write.

The methods and the ethics of this stage of our technology are in rapid flux. Untangling that Gordian knot is far beyond the scope of this work. I'll mention two generic types of programs here. I leave the rest up to you.

Grammar Checkers

Digital grammar checkers can be very helpful tools. The most basic ones check for typos, grammar, and punctuation. More advanced ones can check for readability issues—for example, whether your sentences are too long, or if you repeat the same word too often. You can even tell some applications what genre or type of writing you're working on so it can tailor its suggestions accordingly.

Today, as I work on this manuscript, I have two grammar checkers running. One is built into my word processor, and the other is a free add-on that I find simple and useful. As I draft, I completely ignore both of them. At a later stage, after I have drafted and edited a large section, I use these tools to assist as I proofread.

These programs free me up to focus on the tasks that only I can do. That said, the use of AI grammar checkers has limitations. For one, many writers find them annoying and distracting. They can tempt you to start fussing over details when you should be focusing on the larger issue of what you are attempting to say. It's really hard to share a heartfelt sentiment or a rousing story when a grammar checker is intervening with instructions about verb tense or comma use.

In addition, the suggestions may be inaccurate or inappropriate for your intended reader. You should always review the suggestions carefully to make sure the software isn't introducing new errors, changing your meaning, or implementing changes that don't sound right to the human ear.

My third caution is that over-using grammar checkers will diminish your unique voice. You want to sound like you. There are so many interesting ways to bend the rules for the sake of style, emphasis, or rhythm. Your voice is distinct. Wise authors consider the advice of a grammar checker, writing group, copyeditor, proofreader, or publisher seriously while at the same time reserving final authority for themselves.

Style Checkers

While grammar checkers identify potential errors and make suggestions, a style checker is a different sort of AI program. They can discern readability levels, detect tone, and check for redundancies. They can also produce summaries and outlines, and these can lead to skillful revision. That is the positive side of these AI programs.

Other functions pose potential problems. For example, if you add one popular style checker to your manuscript, it will automatically offer to rewrite your prose, asking "Improve it, make it assertive, shorten it, simplify the vocabulary, or adjust the tone?" While AI tools can be helpful for brainstorming, invasive suggestions can hijack a writer's process and overtake a writer's voice.

Should you use them? Perhaps. In business or marketing, they may help you express your ideas with clarity and vigor. In emails, they may help you find words quickly so you can focus on more important tasks.

However, in school? These style checkers leave the student writer liable for plagiarism. But more importantly, they short-circuit the processes that the classroom experience is intended to teach. They rob students of the chance to develop and rehearse their writing skills. They bypass learning. They prevent you from exercising your skill, the skill that the classroom experience is designed to teach you.

How about in fiction writing? Personal essays? Self-help books? Poetry? To do so raises a host of ethical problems. If it is your name on the cover, what does that mean if AI wrote it? Or rewrote it? Or helped by supplying key content?

Legal and ethical problems aside, computerized style checkers are problematic because they have a homogenizing effect. They undermine the author's nuance and robust individuality. As the use of these tools increases, the human factor—all the things that make your voice unique and put your heart first and foremost on the page—will be increasingly valued. I believe that over time, your personal, distinctive, very human voice will be seen as *priceless*.

Bottom line? Explore the resources available to you through both human and digital editing options. They can become great assistants or dangerous traps. Use them to the extent that they serve to strengthen your unique voice and message.

Pathways to Publishing

If you are considering publishing, it's important to know your options. There are three main models: traditional publishing, self-publishing (aka author publishing), and hybrid publishing.

Traditional publishing is what most people are familiar with. It usually requires you to go through an agent, and it comes with quality, prestige, and an advance. However, many authors are dissatisfied with how little they make when they work with a traditional publisher, how much control they give up, and how little attention their book gets from the publisher if they're not already a big-name author.

Self-publishing, on the other hand, puts all the control in the author's hands. Authors write their book, then they either develop the skills to edit, design, and upload it or they hire support.

It requires lots of time, research, and usually some financial investment, but more and more resources are available to help you do it well.

Hybrid publishing is a mix of the two. You get quality, professional support while retaining significant control. It requires an up-front investment on the author's part, but the author receives higher royalties and a more collaborative experience.

I have done all three, and any one of these can be an excellent fit depending on the project, your needs, and your goals.

Ultimately, if you want to publish, I recommend exploring multiple publishing models and several publishing houses within those models. Each is different. A word of advice: I believe one of the most important aspects of choosing a publisher is having a team that understands and believes in your mission. Interview published authors. Ask what they appreciated and what drawbacks they encountered with their publishers. Before you commit, learn all you can from their experience.

If you have a story to tell or an idea to share, don't neglect the possibilities of publishing electronically. Now don't get me wrong. I love the way a book feels in my hands, and I enjoy having physical copies of published books. Barnes & Noble still provides a haven for people like me. But don't neglect the host of other ways to reach your readers. Blogs, online magazines, or newsletters like Substack are not only great ways to build an audience but also fantastic for establishing good writing habits, getting feedback on your ideas, and developing fluency by meeting regular deadlines. Don't neglect them.

Whatever you decide to do with your completed manuscript, one step is non-negotiable: Take the time to reflect on how far you've come and celebrate all you've accomplished.

When You Write for You

Buried in a box in a dark corner of my closet is a small stack of notebooks filled with poetry. I don't write poetry often, but these little books were produced during a season of distress. I kept trying to make sense of what I was going through by journaling, a practice that I've maintained for decades. But sentences and paragraphs were ill-suited for the tumble of emotions I was feeling. So I decided that if I couldn't figure it out by journaling, I'd see if I could at least name it through poetry. I'll never share these notebooks, and I don't plan to reread them. But in many ways, it is the most important writing I've ever done. Writing bad poetry, as messy and honest and heartfelt as I could manage, became a lifeline through a season when I honestly didn't know how to make it through.

There are lots of forms of writing that need to exist not so much for others, but for yourself. I've written letters with no intention of sending them because I needed the chance to vent. I've written short stories just because the ideas were so vivid or the characters so vibrant that they demanded to be written down. I think of the times I've had a problem to solve or a decision to make; taking the time to make lists and write down my feelings made it all so much clearer.

Wikipedia tells me that publishing is "the process of making information, literature, music, software, and other content, whether in physical or digital form, available to the public." How do you define *available*? What do you mean by *the public*? Shouldn't there be a more capacious view of both these terms? And isn't it possible that the real pleasure of writing, its most potent purpose, has less to do with the distribution of printed works and more to do with the heart?

Chapter 11 Summary
PUBLISH

- The greatest benefit of writing is not publication, sales, or accolades; the greatest benefit is how the writing process shapes the writer.
- A tiny print run may be just right for you.
- Editors specialize. If you choose to hire an editor, make sure to hire the right kind of editor at the right stage of your process, and be specific about the tasks you ask them to complete.
- There are a host of electronic resources available to help with planning, drafting, revising, editing, and proofreading. Some are great; others, not so much. Exercise caution.
- It used to be that the only way to become a published author was to work with a major publishing house. Now, there are a host of options, including self-publishing; hybrid publishers; and small, medium, and large traditional publishing houses.
- Publishing online or creating an e-book may be the best way to reach your readers.
- The most important audience you will ever write for? It's *you.*

The Big Idea

There have never been so many great ways for writers to connect with readers. There has never been a better time to be a writer.

Take a Step

Do a bit of research and consider expanding the possibilities for how you might share your work.

A Final Word

I'll let Anne Lamott sum up:

> I just try to warn people who hope to get published that publication is not all that it is cracked up to be. But writing is. Writing has so much to give, so much to teach, so many surprises. That thing you had to force yourself to do—the actual act of writing—turns out to be the best part.

Chapter 12
THRIVE
Cultivate a More Creative Life

In February of 2006, I received an email from my friend Josh. It was simple enough. It said, "Hey, there's a brand-new book just released that you might find interesting." He included a link to the Amazon page. I didn't think much about it, and I clicked the link.

Turns out, the "brand-new book" that Josh was talking about was *my* book, *The Company They Keep: C. S. Lewis and J. R. R. Tolkien as Writers in Community*. I had been working on that book for more than twenty years. It started as a book report I did in high school. It developed as I gave talks at conferences and published articles in journals. Eventually, it became the subject of my doctoral dissertation, and, after further research and significant revision, it became the book of my heart, the one single work that I am still most proud of.

But here's the point: Even though I had worked on that manuscript for years, I still didn't feel like a writer. I didn't think I was a writer until I clicked the link that Josh sent me. I didn't think I was a writer until I saw my book listed on Amazon.

And *that* was a tragic mistake.

I remember working with artist David Bryan on a huge mural we painted on the side of a barn, visible for many years along the Blue Ridge Highway. We worked long days, and as we painted, we talked a lot about the creative process. I liked his practicality and his New England brevity.

One day, I asked him what it takes to become a painter. He looked at me and said, "Painters paint." And then he went back to work. It annoyed the heck out of me when he said it. But his point was well taken. It was time for me to stop talking about painting, stop thinking about painting, stop buying painting supplies, stop hanging around with painters, stop reading books about painting, and stop trying to figure out some formula for becoming a successful painter. I just needed to get in there and start messing around with paint. Do the thing. Honor the process. Because painters paint.

Painters paint. You know where I am going with this. Writers write. You can expand this to all kinds of categories—sailors sail, runners run, readers read, and skiers ski. Staying actively engaged in doing what we do changes the way we think, the way we dream, the way we spend our time, invest our savings, plan our schedules, and view the world.

The writing life is bigger and broader than merely those times when our fingers fly across the keyboard, and the text takes shape on the screen before us. In this epilogue, the final chapter of *Write Like You Mean It*, I want to talk about cultivating a writer's life.

Keep Refining Your Process

This book offers a big-picture overview of the writing process, and by now, you know that, in some ways, that phrase is misleading since there is no single process for writing. Different writers will develop different processes based on their creative personalities. The process will also change depending on the message, genre, and audience. Specific projects will impose restrictions that limit some options and also create new opportunities.

Not only that, but you will also find that your writing habits change in different seasons of life. When I was in college, I could only write late at night, when everything was quiet, and I could be completely focused. And there was a period in high school when I would go to bed early and then wake at 1:00 a.m., write for a few hours, and then sleep a few hours until morning.

When my daughter was very small, I was working on my book *Clay in the Potter's Hands*. I was utterly exhausted by day's end, and so even though I had never in my life been a morning person, I started to rise at 5:00 a.m. and spend an hour or two typing in my office before Sierra Grace would wake.

These days, my writing life gets scheduled around the academic calendar. I write most mornings before I leave for school, and I schedule longer blocks of time during winter break, spring break, and summer.

Personality, genre, the demands of a particular project, and the seasons of a writer's life—these all give shape to a writer's processes. William Zinsser writes, "There are all kinds of writers and all kinds of methods, and any method that helps you to say what you want to say is the right method for you."

It is true. And yet, having worked with thousands of writers, the concrete steps described in these pages—refocusing, discovering, analyzing, gathering, optimizing, drafting, persisting, revising, editing, proofreading, and thriving—take the mystery out of the process and have proven to be liberating and effective. Experiment. Go on field trips. Read widely. Borrow from the best. You will keep changing, and the details of each step will adapt right alongside you.

Keep Reading About Writing

No matter how long you have been at this, you need a steady diet of new insights and pertinent reminders. We hone our skills by practicing; we expand our capacities by exploring new ideas. There is a bibliography of recommended books at the back of this book, but here are three books that have been life-changing for me.

1. *Bird by Bird: Some Thoughts on Writing and Life* by Anne Lamott
   I asked my writer friends which books on writing they have found to be most helpful. Every one of them mentioned *Bird by Bird.* The basic premise is simple and utterly brilliant. When faced with an overwhelming task, break it down into small steps, then put your head down and take it one step at a time. It is good advice for the writing process. For that matter, it is good advice for any complicated, overwhelming challenge you may be facing.

2. *Creativity: Flow and the Psychology of Discovery and Invention* by Mihaly Csikszentmihalyi
   I used to teach a semester-long course on creativity, and this was our textbook. While many aspects of creativity are elusive, research has a lot to say about what creativity is and how to nurture it. Csikszentmihalyi helped me to demystify the nature of creativity and offers brilliant insight into that magical state called "flow."

3. *The War of Art: Break Through the Blocks and Win Your Inner Creative Battles* by Steven Pressfield
   Sometimes, the thing that trips me up isn't a lack of information or even a lack of inspiration. It's self-doubt. It's second-guessing. It's despair. *The War of Art* describes those demons of resistance that plague us when we attempt any innovation. It's a helpful guide for writers, athletes, artists, entrepreneurs, and others. Need a breakthrough? This book is for you.

If you use social media, search for your favorite authors there. Many use their platforms to share a glimpse of what their lives look like. Some have podcasts or offer classes and webinars; these can be an important investment. Others may speak at conferences or offer book coaching. Follow them, along with any interesting journals, magazines, or bookstores you enjoy. Be on the lookout for interviews, blogs, newsletters, and more, and commit to continuing to read and learn.

Make Writing a Habit

Many writers write sporadically—once every few months, or when inspiration strikes. I am always tempted to write in fits and starts, binging then procrastinating, then binging to finish before the deadline.

But have you noticed it's difficult to get your head back into a project after you've neglected it for a while? You have to remember where you were, what you needed to do, what you wanted to add. I think of the process a blacksmith uses to make a horseshoe. You've seen them, at least in movies, pounding away on that glowing piece of iron, then thrusting it back into the fire until it is red hot, then pounding on it some more. Warm iron can be bent, shaped, refined, reshaped, and renewed. Cold iron will splinter—every time. When we write consistently, we keep the iron of our creativity red hot, ready to be shaped and fashioned. I think about this image when I am in the midst of a writing project.

I learned this from Joseph Bentz. When I see him, I ask, "How is the writing coming?"

He smiles and always gives me the same answer. "Every day until it's done."

Every day until it's done. Joe is somewhat notorious in our circle of friends for this well-established habit. Once he reaches a certain phase of the writing process—he has a strong idea, he is excited about it, and he has gathered a folder full of the content he will need—he starts drafting, and while he is drafting, he works faithfully. Every day. Until the draft is done.

How serious is he? This commitment to write every day included the morning his wife went into labor. "How long until we need to go to the hospital?" he asked her.

"Oh, probably a couple of hours, I guess."

Joe sat down at the computer and worked on the next chapter of his novel, fingers flying across the keyboard.

Some circumstances and situations pull us away from our work, but I honor the principle Joe lives by. Like that ironworker, the writer needs to keep their material warm and pliable. The writer needs to keep the project moving forward, and one way to do that is to work on it a little bit every day.

Dillard uses a wonderful metaphor to illustrate the principle:

> A work in progress quickly becomes feral. It reverts to a wild state overnight. It is barely domesticated, a mustang on which you one day fastened a halter, but which now you cannot catch. It is a lion you cage in your study. As the work grows, it gets harder to control; it is a lion growing in strength. You must visit it every day and reassert your mastery over it. If you skip a day, you are, quite rightly, afraid to open the door to its room. You enter its room with bravura, holding a chair at the thing and shouting, "Simba!"

The habit of writing daily is a favorite bit of advice. From Stephen King: "If I don't write every day, the characters begin to stale off in my mind—they begin to seem like characters instead of real people." From Ray Bradbury: "You must stay drunk on writing so reality cannot destroy you.... Just write every day of your Life." And from Steven Pressfield: "'Turning pro' means adopting professional habits: showing up daily regardless of mood or inspiration."

Writing every day does not necessarily mean increasing the word count. It may mean doing background reading, editing a section, drafting an illustration, gathering quotations, or checking a bibliographic entry. I have found that it doesn't matter what I do or how long I spend doing it as long as I stay actively engaged with the material. If I want to keep the project moving forward, I need to make at least a little progress most every day.

This type of consistency does not rely on inspiration, but on schedule and routine. The secret is not *finding* time but *making* time and ruthlessly defending it. As author Ralph Keyes puts it, "Serious writers write.... Over time, they discover that routine is a better friend than inspiration." Routines have a way of signaling to our brain that it needs to enter a certain mode. The more you establish the habit of writing, the easier it becomes to "get in the zone."

But how do you stay faithful to those habits and routines? Create accountability measures that motivate you. A productive writing life includes setting goals, blocking time in your schedule, and rewarding yourself. It's a matter of good habits. You can involve others, like a writing group or a check-in system, to help you stay on track.

One simple trick helps me maintain momentum when I am working on a long-term project. I keep a list of dates and the total word count of my project in the upper-right corner of the first page of my document. As I am wrapping up today's writing session, the top of page one looks something like this:

22 Dec 68,038
21 Dec 67,207
20 Dec 66,891
19 Dec 67,441
17 Dec 66,605
16 Dec 63,162
14 Dec 63,016

As you think about applying this, remember that consistency has many forms. Paul J. Silvia recommends finding four hours a week. Jeff Goins suggests five hundred words a day. I try to write six days a week. I don't always make it.

By the way, I don't mind when the word count shrinks. In fact, that probably means I've done some important cutting (remember Airport Man). A lowered word count often means significant progress.

Ultimately, for me, the number of words isn't the most important thing; the list of dates is. Did I open the document and work on it at least a little bit on most days? I follow the advice of James Clear, author of *Atomic Habits*. I keep a running record, and then I am motivated to keep working because I don't want to "break the chain." It is satisfying to see the number of words grow from one hundred to one thousand or more. But what really brings me joy is seeing consistency. Bit by bit. It's true. Line by line. Baby steps will get you there.

Find what creative rhythm works for you. Follow the advice of Paul J. Silvia: "Let everyone else procrastinate, daydream, and complain—spend your time sitting down and moving your mittens."

Invest Strategically

One of my favorite photographs is a picture of me that was taken in a large furniture store. I was headed toward the couches when I spied a beautiful woodgrain desk and stopped dead in my tracks. It was love at first sight. The grain, the burnished dark brown color, the rustic texture. Love, love, love.

My friend took a picture of the moment on her phone. I think she might have done it to make fun of me. I mean, who falls in love with a piece of furniture? But seeing that desk led me to make a life-changing choice. I decided then and there that my work as a writer mattered. I knew I needed to start making strategic investments in my writing life.

Here's what that looked like for me. I decided to keep my old couch and manage without a washer or dryer for the time being. I took all the money I had saved up for home improvements, and I used it to buy that desk instead. For weeks, I would wake up in the morning, remember that beautiful desk, and smile. This morning, years later, when I sat down at my desk in my office to write this paragraph, I smiled again.

Postponing other purchases and investing in a beautiful desk was worth it to me. I feel sustained, even joyful, and I find that this specific decision has repaid me many times over.

Maybe it isn't a desk that inspires you. Maybe it is having a full dozen of your favorite pens, a ream of quality paper for your printer, a nice hardcover journal, or a fresh filing system with matching magazine boxes to organize your research notes. A better chair? An ergonomic keyboard? A hardcover copy of your favorite book, some colored sticky notes, or a monogram embosser? Anything, from scented candles to a handmade coffee mug, might lift your mood and make long hours at the writing desk just a little more welcoming.

Don't get me wrong. I am not advocating for a burdensome splurge or a shopping spree. I am encouraging you to think about how you might adjust your budget to make room to invest strategically in your writing life. Nourish your writing life by being aware of the ways that a few curated indulgences will take the edge off the hard labor of writing consistently and help you find extra pleasure in the process.

Attend Writers' Conferences

A friend of mine pestered me year after year to start attending writers' conferences, and I resisted. Didn't have the time. Couldn't spend that much money. Didn't like to travel. Anyway, I figured that writing conferences were a big extravagance just to pick up a handful of tips to help improve my writing.

I was wrong.

My first writers' conference was worth its weight in gold. New friends. Outstanding encouragement. Renewed energy. And a whole new vision of research, writing, and publishing. Going to my first writers' conference was crucial for me. It was the one thing that did the most to help me transition from being a writer to becoming an author. It changed me for good.

There are many kinds of writing conferences, big and small, local and international, virtual and in-person. Most have a special emphasis, maybe a particular genre like mystery writers, or maybe an aspect of writing like editing or marketing.

Take the time to discover conferences that suit your interests, needs, and budget. The right writers' conference might be the best investment you could make.

Schedule Writing Retreats

A big part of lifelong productivity is knowing yourself, and here is one thing I know for sure about my work as a writer. I can edit, do a little research, or complete other microtasks practically any time of day and pretty much anywhere. But when it comes to drafting, it is harder for me to invoke my creative Muse. I need longer, uninterrupted blocks of time. I find that writing retreats are a necessity.

My first book offers an inside look at the collaboration of Lewis, Tolkien, and the Inklings. I wanted to tell the story of what these guys said to each other and what difference it made to the books they were writing. The challenge for me was two-fold. First, I had a full-time job and a busy family. Second, this project required me to juggle an enormous amount of complex material while writing it up in a clear, straightforward way.

Here's how I did it. I scheduled writing retreats. I would bring food, clothes, and writing supplies. I would check into a hotel and get to work. I would draft as fast as I could and work as hard as I was able. When I checked out of the hotel the next day, I took myself out to lunch, where I sat and created a list of the next steps, microtasks that could be completed in fifteen minutes or less, such as look up that scholar's name, find that quote about the mouse, and rewrite that story about how much Lewis disliked Tolkien when they first met.

The blessing for me was creating an oasis of time during which I had only one single thing to do—make progress on the manuscript. Move the project forward. No dishes to wash, emails to answer, bills to pay, papers to grade, lessons to plan. Just write as much as I can.

Then I'd head back home, back into my busy life, back into trying to find a few minutes a day, every day, so I could continue to make progress. My goal was to cross one task off my list every day and to find one or two longer blocks of time each week to complete some serious writing. And head for another retreat in three or four months.

I still find writing retreats to be profoundly helpful when I am in the drafting stage. Drafting demands my best attention, my most alert and focused self. I've gone on weekend retreats, week-long retreats, private retreats, and group retreats. Sometimes, I've managed to add a writing day (sometimes two) to a trip taken for another purpose. This provides a fresh environment and a bit of focused, uninterrupted time.

While these types of retreats may not seem realistic, retreats come in many attainable forms. It needn't be overnight, and it doesn't have to be costly. On some writing days, I'll schedule a full day to spend at the library, with a break for lunch at a favorite restaurant. A morning at a coffee shop, a long afternoon in the park, the guest room at a friend's house, or an inexpensive overnight at a retreat center or monastery. Be creative. Consider options.

The magic seems to kick in when I change the venue. These fresh spaces and long, quiet, focused, uninterrupted hours help me outpace procrastination and the monsters of doubt, indecision, perfectionism, distraction, and worry, and just *write*. Write as if my life depended on it. Write as quickly as I can. As badly as I dare.

Invite Others on the Journey

I'll say it again: One of the most pernicious lies about the creative process is that it is lonely and solitary. The Hollywood version of a productive writer depicts a lone individual, typing away in a cabin in the woods (yikes) or alone late at night, wadding up sheets of paper and throwing them into an overflowing wastebasket.

Writers do make time to focus their attention, and often, they really do work alone, but should writers be isolated? Heavens, no. Writing is transactional, and that assumes at least two people—a writer and a reader. And the writing process itself is enriched and enhanced when we are intentional about involving others along the way.

How can we invite others alongside us? Here are four main ways.

Critique Groups

I've studied the writing process of successful writers for decades, trying to understand the secret of their productivity and the lasting impact of their books. What have I come across time and time again? The power of critique groups—groups that read each other's work and offer substantial feedback to make it better.

When Lewis and Tolkien met with their writing group, the Inklings, they spent time in conversation, asking about projects, trying out ideas, and supporting and challenging each other. They met every Thursday—an unvarying schedule which fostered accountability. Meetings began the same way: some small talk, a pot of strong, black tea, and then Lewis would call the meeting to order. "Well?" he would say. "Has nobody got anything to read us?"

The Inklings spent most of their weekly meetings reading and critiquing their work-in-progress. Tolkien's *Lord of the Rings* was written this way, chapter by chapter, week after week. So were dozens of other works, such as Lewis's *Screwtape*

Letters, Warren Lewis's *Splendid Century,* Charles Williams' *All Hallows' Eve,* and so many more. Books that have become some of the best-selling titles of the twentieth century were forged in that sitting room in Oxford.

The Inklings and groups like it have continued to inspire writers to discover their best work by making the connection. When Abigail wanted more support, she posted on social media to find others interested in joining her. A writing group took shape, and they have been meeting on Zoom every other Tuesday since 2021.

In these meetings, someone prepares a creative writing exercise for the group. "Write a poem based on this painting." "Pull two words out of a jar and use them in a story." "Write about a childhood memory from someone else's perspective." There is a pressure to write quickly that creates a sense of abandon, an urgency to make decisions without overthinking. As they complete warm-up exercises, then read their work out loud and talk about the writer's craft, they flex their creative imagination. These regular times together offer more than support and companionship; they help each participant exercise and develop their skills.

Since this group's start, many of the members have begun writing books, with a built-in community for discussion, support, and celebration. All have ventured to try types of writing they never would have otherwise, standing together against the forces of doubt, hesitation, and perfectionism.

Coffee Conversations

A critique group is somewhat structured and requires someone to offer their unfinished draft for feedback. Some writers would sooner toss their laptop into the ocean. And sometimes the writing is still taking shape, not yet ready for critique.

Happily, there are other ways to get support that don't involve reading one another's work. The simplest and most effective way is a coffee conversation—talking to someone about what you're writing and what's got you stuck. Make time to hang out with friends who are interested in your topic or curious about the story you are working on.

Talking about the work face-to-face has a way of blasting through writer's block. Connecting with potential readers often offers a course correction, providing new energy and vision. Even speaking with friends who are not fellow writers can be helpful for perspective on the project and for returning to it refreshed.

There is a group of friends I know who have a truly impressive record of academic publications. While the rest of us are moseying along, these guys seem to publish something new every month or two. Their secret? Their local coffee shop, twice a week. Like clockwork.

Let me explain. Part one of their secret is schedule and routine. These writers plan and coordinate their work schedules so they have two full mornings each week dedicated to writing. They get up early, and they write as much as they can as fast as they can. Then they meet late in the morning for coffee.

They don't have to take time to decide whether today is a writing day. It's already built into the calendar. They don't have to wonder how to prioritize the tasks of the day. It's already written down. In short, it would take a conscious decision and a concerted effort to neglect the plan for the day. They get up in the morning, and they sit down to write. Routine, place, time, and habit are automatic. It's built in.

Part two of their secret is accountability. These guys are competitive to the bone, and no one wants to show up for coffee and admit they spent the morning surfing the web or flipping through a magazine. They want to show up and show off what they have done.

But the most important part of their secret, part three, is conversation. Have you ever spent the morning working on a story, article, blog post, or book chapter, and no matter how much effort you put into it, you couldn't figure out how to say the thing that was locked deep inside?

These writers spend their coffee hour trying to explain to each other what they are trying to say in whatever they are working on. "I am trying to explain why Plato prefigures belief in the supernatural," one will say. "I am trying to get my main character introduced to the man who will become his mentor," says another.

And here's where the magic happens. Someone in the group will say, "Tell me more about that," or ask, "Well, what *are* you trying to say?"

"What are you trying to say?" It's a simple question with enormous generative power. I cannot count the number of times I have been stuck on a project until a friend asks me what I am trying to say. The words pour forth like a waterfall. Writer's block is demolished. I race back to my keyboard and scramble to write it all down.

Here's why coffee conversations work so well. People are designed to communicate face to face. Our brains are wired to generate language more easily in the presence of another human. Having coffee with a caring, interested listener isn't just a morale boost; it engages systems in our brains that go dormant when we sit alone at a notebook or laptop. That's why it's often easier to explain something to a friend than it is to sit down and write a cohesive paragraph while staring at the computer screen. Even introverts find sharper focus, better words, clearer thoughts, and more adrenaline when they are asked, face to face, "What are you trying to say?"

There's more. When we gather, we see the effect of our ideas on others as they listen and respond. When these academics describe their projects to one another, they may see nods of agreement or hear a word of praise that confirms they are on the right track. Or they may see confusion, tension, concern, or distraction. That suggests the need to regroup, rethink, and try a different tack.

After coffee? These guys race back to the project with greater clarity, new insights, strong encouragement, and renewed faith. They can't wait to report back the next time they meet for coffee so they can tell the others just how far they've come.

Accountability

Writers don't like deadlines, but we need them. We invariably write better when a due date looms. It is enormously clarifying. Energizing. Focusing. Critique groups and coffee conversations work well, but there are other accountability strategies that also make a huge difference.

Some writers I know simply text each other at the end of each day to say how many words they have written. No message, just a number. 230. 452. 1,922. Some writers love the accountability; others thrive when faced with healthy competition.

While drafting this book, I posted regular progress reports on Facebook. I had set a very ambitious goal to get the first draft done quickly. So, from time to time, I'd post my daily word count and also my total word count, like this: "TODAY 1,298. TOTAL 23,561." The process of writing this book was sustained by hundreds of friends who liked those reports and responded by posting words of encouragement. Even better, many friends who were following the report took the time to reach out personally and ask me about the project. Thank you, thank you, Facebook friends. I continue to be supported and motivated as you cheer my successes and encourage me through doubts, setbacks, frustrations, second thoughts, hard days, and utter failures.

Practical Help

There is a story about Lewis and Tolkien that always brings me to the verge of tears. They were trying to make progress on their various writing projects during the shadow of the Second World War. That meant shortages of every kind: sugar, meat, tires, gasoline, coffee, butter, canned goods, and shoes. Lewis, Tolkien, and the other Inklings struggled with all of these restrictions. But the shortage that hit them the hardest? They ran out of paper.

Paper. We take it for granted; they couldn't find paper anywhere. So they made it a habit to save up scraps—the back of an envelope, say, or a sheet only partially used. They would bring these scraps to their weekly meetings. Those who had extra paper gave what they had. Those who had little would gratefully receive this priceless gift. Priceless? I think so. In the days before computers, no writer could write without it.

Practical help. Maybe it's providing writing supplies or offering a quiet place to work. Or watching kids for a couple of hours, making a run to the grocery store, delivering a Venti cup of coffee, or arranging for a delivery service to show up at the door with dinner. Maybe it's pitching in to fix a computer glitch, sharing a helpful book, or sitting around brainstorming titles.

And then there is the practical help of networking, connecting that writer to publishers, subject experts, marketing specialists, editors, collaborators, mentors, and friends.

Try planning a book launch, placing a pre-order, leaving an Amazon review, or sharing the book on your social media.

No doubt you can think of a dozen other ways to help other writers. Or to ask for the kind of practical help you need.

As we invest in each other, we all benefit. Companions on the journey make our burdens lighter and open up the possibilities before us. Companions on the journey make it possible for each one of us to do what we were born to do.

MAGIC TRICK

Parallel Play

When the world was in lockdown during the pandemic, I faced one of the most challenging seasons of my life. Isolated at home, I taught classes online. Technology is not my favorite. Being away from the classroom and my students is most definitely not my favorite. Since I didn't need to travel to school, I had more time on my hands. You would think I'd get a lot more writing done. But I was sad and lonely, and that sucked out every last drop of my creative energy. It was a slog.

Here's what transformed that experience: parallel play.

"Parallel play," or co-working, is when people gather and work simultaneously on independent projects. Picture students studying different topics as they sit together in the library. Meeting up with a writer friend at a coffee shop while you each work on your own prose. Or perhaps co-working at your desk while linked together on a video call. That's what I did.

You see, my friend Hannah was making great progress on her novel, and I was working hard on a book called *The Major and the Missionary.* We set up a schedule: Every Wednesday at 8:30 a.m., we would connect on Zoom. We'd briefly report on what we had accomplished in the past week. We would describe what we would be working on this particular morning. Then we'd say a prayer and start to write. Not together. Not talking and not collaborating. Zoom was on; the sound was off. We'd spend three hours together, each of us working as hard as we could to make as much progress as possible in those three hours.

"Companions on the journey make it possible for each one of us to do what we were born to do.

Why did this work so well? Knowing that Hannah was hard at work kept me in the chair and on task. At other times and on other days, I was always tempted to wander off, check social media, make a coffee, grab a snack, wash a few dishes, or walk the dog. But during that three-hour block of time, I wrote. And so did Hannah.

After our writing time was done, we'd briefly report on what we had accomplished. We'd articulate our specific goals for the next week. And we'd look forward to next Wednesday and our next writing session together.

Here is the truth: I got more written in that three-hour block of parallel play than I did the rest of the week put together.

If you don't have someone available for parallel play, create your own group. One of my colleagues has a super busy schedule, but he really wants to make progress on the book he is writing. When he finds he has a little time—a free hour or two—he texts a group of friends and invites them to gather on Zoom. He's got poets, artists, scholars, movie makers, and storytellers who show up. In less than a year, his group is not only varied, robust, and productive, but it's also international.

Why does it work so well? The presence of another person provides accountability to stay off your phone. You don't want to let the others down. Having another person present may also remind you that there will be a real person reading your work, which helps you focus on how best to communicate. We are social beings—it may simply make the writing process more enjoyable (and therefore more sustainable) to work beside a friend. I cannot say enough about the magic of parallel play.

Writers Write

What comes next as we come to the end of this book? In Chapter 6, I encouraged you to write as fast as you can and as badly as you dare. I told you to take action. "Write generously. Put thoughts into words. Put images into descriptions. Put scenes into action. Put lines into poetry."

Take action. Remember, writers write. That's the heart of the process. That's the essence of the work. Murray puts it this way: "Writing is primarily not a matter of talent, of dedication, of vision, of vocabulary, of style, but simply a matter of sitting. The writer is a person who writes."

As we mentioned, Flannery O'Connor was committed to this habit. She writes, "Every morning between 9 and 12 I go to my room and sit before a piece of paper."

Murray adds, "She was a magnificent sitter; I wish I could sit as well as Flannery O'Connor." So do I. So do I.

You sit. You stay. You breathe. You listen. You gather a few ideas, and you write a line or two. You suddenly remember that quotation from that one guy, and you write it down. You check your notes, recall a conversation, take another deep breath, a phrase comes into focus, and you write some more.

Good day? Bad day? Busy day? Hard day? That's okay.

Don't feel like writing? That's okay, too.

Sit yourself down.

Do it anyway.

Take the next step.

Make the time.

Write like you mean it: Let the words and ideas and images and stories that are locked in your imagination start to show up on the page.

Write like you mean it: Let your authentic self, your vision, your dreams, your way of being in this world be reflected clearly by saying what it is that only you can say.

Write like you mean it: It's time to buckle down and take your gifts seriously.

Like you mean it: Believe in yourself.

Like you mean it: Because it matters.

Pick up your pen.

Grab your journal.

Reach for the keyboard.

Write.

Chapter 12 Summary
THRIVE

- Keep learning and developing new habits.
- Make strategic investments to create a great space and equip your imagination.
- Consider conferences and retreats.
- Let go of the idea of the solitary genius and build a robust circle of support.
- Connect with others to energize your writing, build in accountability, and get practical help.
- Parallel play will change your life.
- Remember: Writers write.

The Big Idea

Creative breakthroughs and lifelong productivity are fueled by small, strategic action steps that you take as you devote time, invest resources, and give priority to your work as a writer.

Take a Step

Reach out to a friend and schedule some time to get together. Dream up potential projects and brainstorm ideas for one or two specific steps to help you get started.

A Final Word

We can take small steps, build durable habits, and enjoy a more creative, productive life.

Appendix
Encouragement for Publishers, Book Coaches, Teachers, and Writing Centers

Write Like You Mean It isn't just for professional writers. It draws on decades of classroom experience and provides a proven pathway to help reluctant writers get motivated to write. Each step can be easily adapted into a system to help you, step by step, as you supervise others as they make their way through writing projects.

The Pathway Approach strives to demystify the writing process. It provides a sweeping overview of the journey from a vague idea to a finished, polished manuscript, offering concrete, practical advice every step of the way. As I explain in Chapter 1, most writing advice presents writers with two problems.

First, it tends to focus on what the final product is supposed to look like rather than offering systematic strategies for making steady progress through the process. In *The Elements of Style*, for example, Strunk and White offer terrific advice about the characteristics of good written prose. But writers who struggle need specific guidance that explains where to start and then how to overcome obstacles and complete that project.

Second, it lacks a clear and flexible system. Books on the writing process mention the need to prewrite, write, and rewrite. This book builds on that time-tested advice by breaking down the general steps into concrete tasks and providing guidance that is actionable.

As you sit down to support a ninth-grader who is struggling with a research paper, a Master's student who can't seem to pull together her research into a coherent thesis, or a novelist whose story keeps getting longer and longer with no end in sight, you may wonder how to help. The clear structure, powerful questions, and practical action-oriented advice in these pages will help you as you lead them to real results.

Write Like You Mean It can help fledgling writers find their voice and seasoned writers refine their work habits. And you can adapt this system as you come alongside and coach them through it.

Learn the specific questions that help writers turn their topic into a message. Analyze the habits—time, place, materials, methods—that work best for them as they write. Help them enrich their content through interviews, field trips, and reliable research. Show them the magic of a horrible, no good, very bad first draft. Teach them to revise the content and structure before they fiddle with the details of grammar.

I believe that *Write Like You Mean It* can help any writer improve their writing process and hone their writing skills. Many will read it and succeed. This book provides a clear path that will sustain writers as they overcome fear, confusion, and overwhelm, and make steady progress on the project they long to complete.

But many writers need the help that comes from a guide on the side, not a sage on the page. That's where your voice, your encouragement, and your sincere investment in their talent come into play.

One of the most helpful aspects of this book for writing teachers and coaches is that it provides a clear vocabulary for providing targeted feedback and identifying next steps. And it prioritizes that vocabulary based on the writer's stage in the process.

Think about the value of using language like this to guide the writers you work with:

- You need to clarify your audience and adjust your vocabulary to suit them.
- You are still just repeating your claims without elaboration or support.
- I like the ideas here, but they need to be adjusted to meet the demands of this genre.

- How will you schedule your time to achieve your writing goals?
- Your content is thin. How might a field trip or interview add new information?
- Have you checked with a librarian to locate more scholarly sources?
- This draft is great! Now let's work on the sequence of your ideas.

You can use *Write Like You Mean It* to identify specific strengths to praise and articulate specific tasks to complete.

I sincerely hope you will find this book a helpful guide. The work you do is hard, and I would be thrilled to know that this book has equipped you to equip others.

Acknowledgments

Find a group of people who challenge
and inspire you, spend a lot of time with them,
and it will change your life forever.
Amy Poehler

From Diana Pavlac Glyer

Sierra Grace, the light of my life. You have had to put up with nonstop writing projects since the day you were born. Thank you, Sierra, that after all this time, you continue to support my work and believe in me.

The Ninos, my writing group, has steadied my steps and prayed for miracles. I could not do what I do without you.

I am forever grateful to my colleagues in the Honors College at Azusa Pacific University, especially to founding dean **David Weeks,** who invited me ages ago to edit a small book on the liberal arts in higher education. It was the foundation of so much that was to come. Dr. Weeks also supported me as I developed a summer Teaching Writing Workshop for faculty and a lecture series for undergraduates that supports their growth as writers and scholars. The seeds of *Write Like You Mean It* were sown through those challenging and generous opportunities.

Courtney Heidorn, my research assistant. Every week, you did more than expected and at a far higher level than I had any right to ask. Your skill and patience made a substantial contribution to this manuscript. I'm delighted we've had the chance to work together.

Lancia: Where would I be without you, sister-of-my-heart.

Andrew and Christin Lazo: For feedback, encouragement, and sustaining prayer. Andrew: You have books in you, lots of books, important books. I want to read them. You need to write them.

Cecilia, Stan, Kona, and Baxter: I drafted and revised many of these chapters during quiet mornings at Twin Creek Ranch. Your kindness and tender care have been a source of joy and strength. Your friendship is such a delight. Say "hi" to the Umbrellies for me. I am more grateful than I can say.

Brae and Jill Wyckoff, and all of the other good people at Kingdom Writers Association, who prayed for me through the challenge of making this book a reality.

Adam and Becky Bradley: You make my life better, and that shines through in the work I do. I love you.

Beta Readers: Megan Keesler, Joseph Bentz, Sørina Higgins, Teresa Johnston, Michael Dean Clark, Jordyn Fouts, and Mia Guillen. Creativity thrives in community. How glad I am for the ways you have come alongside and made this book far better.

Becky Rickett, the website you created is truly a thing of beauty, and it is a joy to work with you.

Caedon Spilman, I am continuously delighted by your imagination and creativity. You make beautiful things.

From Abigail Stone

I adore my work as an editor and book coach. I get to be a midwife of messages! What sacred work. But amid so many creative projects, it can be challenging to invest in one's own. For that reason, I'm incredibly grateful to the many people in my life who have consistently affirmed my identity as both an editor and a writer, teaching me about the creative process and helping me see it through.

First, thanks to God, who made me (and you!) as a creative being and who invites us to work by His side.

Thank you, **Erik**, for loving me without condition, for bearing witness to all the raw and unedited versions of myself, and for keeping me well-fed and caffeinated.

To **my parents**, you were the first ones to show me that my words mattered. Thank you for cheering on my every passion and for giving me my pen name.

My dear friends, **Ashley Jones, Meghan Parsons, Angela Whitfield, Maris Gentry, Carlyn Hawkinson, Katy Siedentopp,** you call me back to my truest self. I can do anything by your side.

To my **Radiant Youth** team, thank you for tending my soul and showering me with your prayers.

I'm grateful to the **Azusa Pacific University Writing Center**, the job that made me realize I'd be happy if I could spend the rest of my life helping people write.

Carmen Berry, I can't thank you enough for taking me under your wing as a recent grad and including me in your vision. You taught me the creative process, stretched my tolerance for the unknown, and introduced me to the industry that is now my home.

Thank you to the **Independent Book Publishers Association** for stoking my fascination and welcoming me into a community of innovators who make book dreams a reality.

To every person who has been part of my **Pen Pals** community, you have been the safe place I needed to take off my editor hat, defy perfectionism, and reclaim the joy of the craft. Thank you for your vulnerability, creativity, and friendship.

To **every author** I have worked with, collaboration with you has filled me with immeasurable joy. When I see you write the words only you can write, I know I am doing what I was made to do.

Finally

The Berry Powell Team: **Carolyn Rafferty, Marianne Croonquist, Kay McConnaughey**—and to our copyeditor, **Valeri Mills Barnes.** Thank you for your belief in this project and your collaboration through the process. Your talent, faith, and hard work made this dream a reality.

Recommended Reading

Books are a uniquely portable magic.
Stephen King

Bird by Bird: Some Instructions on Writing and Life
by Anne Lamott
This book appears on pretty much every single list anywhere that gathers "my favorite books about writing." It's one of my top ten favorite books in *any* genre. It's brilliant.

Steal Like an Artist by Austin Kleon
This is a book for those times when you are too tired to read. No, I'm serious. Kleon's work is more like an artistic little scrapbook of inspiration, ideas, and fun. I keep *Steal Like an Artist* and its sequel, *Keep Going*, lying around the house. When I am attacked by writer's block or bleary-eyed from spending too many hours in a row staring at the computer screen, I read a few pages, and everything changes.

Talk to Me: How to Ask Better Questions, Get Better Answers, and Interview Anyone Like a Pro by Dean Nelson
The idea of interviewing may sound appealing, but how do you actually get the interview you want without looking silly? Nelson draws on decades of experience and offers practical tools and encouragement to help you craft smarter questions and build real rapport.

A Writer's Reference by Diana Hacker
Many writers are fascinated with details of grammar, usage, and citation systems. I am not one of them. I rely on great resources to correct my blind spots and support me as I work hard to get the details right. When I need it, my favorite reference book is this best-selling textbook by Diana Hacker.

Bandersnatch: C. S. Lewis, J. R. R. Tolkien, and the Creative Collaboration of the Inklings by Diana Pavlac Glyer
Sometimes it's great to have someone summarize and declare the key principles of writing and creativity. But, on the other hand, sometimes we need an inside look at how other writers do what they do. *Bandersnatch* tells the story of the highly interactive, sometimes contentious process that C. S. Lewis, J. R. R. Tolkien, and the Inklings followed as they helped each other write some of the most important books of the last century.

The Craft of Revision by Donald M. Murray
Studying with Don Murray at the University of New Hampshire changed my life. *Write Like You Mean It* owes everything to Don for his good sense, his emphasis on process over product, his daybooks, his optimism, and his determination to pass along everything he knew for the benefit of others.

Creativity, Inc. by Ed Catmull
Pixar keeps rolling out innovative and beautifully crafted films. This book describes their philosophy of creativity and, in inspiring and compelling terms, explains why they are so good at what they do.

100 Ways to Improve Your Writing by Gary Provost
Sometimes I don't need a lot of words and a bunch of complicated advice. I need a suggestion or two. Provost's book is always on hand on the shelf above my desk.

Plot & Structure by James Scott Bell
If you are writing fiction, you absolutely must get your hands on the work of James Scott Bell. In addition to *Plot & Structure*, I recommend *The Last 50 Pages* and his lecture series *How to Write Best-Selling Fiction*, part of The Great Courses (formerly known as The Teaching Company).

Atomic Habits by James Clear
One of my favorite books. Period. I reread *Atomic Habits* regularly because I need to keep reminding myself of two key ideas: Small steps make a big difference, and once something becomes a habit, it becomes effortless. This is one of the first books I recommend to my college freshmen. It is also one of the first books that I hand to my graduate students.

Craft in the Real World by Matthew Salesses
Salesses challenges the traditionally narrow lens through which the writing craft is often taught. In its place, he offers a more expansive vision of the craft that honors diverse perspectives and lived experiences. At its core is his powerful assertion: "When we write fiction, we write the world."

Creativity: Flow and the Psychology of Discovery and Invention by Mihaly Csikszentmihalyi
I used to teach a semester-long course on creativity, and this was our textbook. While many aspects of creativity seem magical or elusive, there is a lot we do know about it. I'm grateful for the way this book articulates a multitude of factors guaranteed to enhance our creative process.

On Writing by Stephen King
Part memoir and part practical advice, *On Writing* is an invitation to look inside the writing process of one of the world's most prolific and successful writers.

Notes

p. xiii "choose to collaborate." For more insight into how writers can collaborate effectively, learn from the example of a famous writing group known as the Inklings. See *Bandersnatch* by Diana Pavlac Glyer.

PART ONE: Start Strong

Chapter 1 REFOCUS: Transform Your Writing

p. 3 "Say what you mean" (J. Miller) The "16 Rules" commonly attributed to Vonnegut were compiled and circulated by John J. Miller. They draw on Vonnegut's "Creative Writing 101" guidelines in *Bagombo Snuff Box* (9–10) and his essay "How to Write with Style" in *Palm Sunday* (65–72).

pp. 3–4 "a few of [Annie Dillard's] guidelines" (Chee).

p. 4 "Use the active voice" (Strunk and White 18–23).

p. 4 "Good writing is lean" (Zinsser 70–71).

p. 4 "write as truthfully as possible" (King 148).

p. 4 "Write straight into the emotional center" (Lamott 226).

p. 5 "Never use two words when one will do" (Jefferson).

p. 5 "Leave out the parts that people skip" (Leonard).

p. 5 "When you catch an adjective, kill it" (Twain).

p. 5 "the glint of light on broken glass" (Chekhov).

p. 6 “a compelling vision” (Comer 158).

p. 7 “Mrs. Appleyard” is the pen name of Louise Andrews Kent, the celebrated author who wrote the Mrs. Appleyard cookbooks, featuring classic, homey recipes and Vermont life. Lauralee adapted Kent’s recipe for her extraordinary four-layer cake.

p. 10 “Murakami’s writing routine” (Currey).

p. 11 “How many iterations it goes through” (Csikszentmihalyi 80–81).

p. 11 The *Paris Review* interviews have been published in a four-volume set and are also available at www.theparisreview.org/interviews.

Chapter 2 DISCOVER: Find Your Path

p. 20 “stare at me as I write.” Science fiction writer Harlan Ellison (1934–2018) was famous for performing live, improvised writing sessions while sitting in the front windows of bookstores. The stunt reliably drew a big crowd. He would set up a manual typewriter at a desk and start a story, often pausing to ask for input. When he finished a page, he would tape it to the window for folks to read. Some of his most popular short stories were written this way. He said he did it to rebuke the belief that writing is mystical, and to emphasize it’s a task like any other task, “like being a plumber or an electrician” (Palmer).

p. 21 “this one-draft view of writing” (Harris 99).

Chapter 3 ANALYZE: Define Your Task

p. 27 "Preparation precedes power" (Hinckley 42).

p. 30 "Each genre has its own peculiar set of expectations." For an in-depth look at genres, see *The Anatomy of Genres* by John Truby. For an introduction to genre theory, listen to Truby's interview on the podcast *Friends & Fiction*, available on apple podcasts.

p. 31 "If you want to be a writer" (King 145).

p. 31 "I'm a slow reader" (King 145).

p. 31 "Every book you pick up" (King 145).

p. 31 "Read a lot and read widely." A note for students: If you are struggling with a classroom writing assignment, ask your teacher or your school's Writing Center if they have some sample papers you might look at. It is much easier to write a paper if you have an idea of what the finished product is supposed to look like.

p. 32 "only great power" (*The Hobbit*).

pp. 33–34 "What is a legacy?" (Miranda).

Chapter 4 GATHER: Stockpile Ideas

p. 43 "What if?" (Lackey qtd. in Klein).

p. 44 "You sweep" (Lee).

p. 44 "Every morning" ("250 Quotes by Flannery O'Connor").

p. 44 "with a club" (London).

p. 46 "I write entirely to find out what I'm thinking" (Didion).

p. 46 "ideas are everywhere" (McPhee).

p. 47 "storing things away" (Lamott 66).

p. 47 "Good story ideas" (King 37).

p. 49 "the most popular reference website" ("History of Wikipedia").

p. 50 "It's hard for me" (King 147).

p. 50 "write creatively" (Csikszentmihalyi 47).

p. 51 "contribute your verse." I like to think of the writing we do as a contribution to the ongoing conversation. I have been strongly influenced by the perspective of Kenneth Burke, who writes: "Imagine that you enter a parlor. You come late. When you arrive, others have long preceded you, and they are engaged in a heated discussion, a discussion too heated for them to pause and tell you exactly what it is about. In fact, the discussion had already begun long before any of them got there, so that no one present is qualified to retrace for you all the steps that had gone before. You listen for a while, until you decide that you have caught the tenor of the argument; then you put in your oar. Someone answers; you answer him; another comes to your defense; another aligns himself against you, to either the embarrassment or gratification of your opponent, depending upon the quality of your ally's assistance. However, the discussion is interminable. The hour grows late, you must depart. And you do depart, with the discussion still vigorously in progress" (Burke 110–11). As writers, we are never speaking in a vacuum. We are entering a conversation that has been going on for a long, long time and will continue long after.

p. 51 "Librarians are just like search engines" (Haig).

p. 54 "ventured to the top of the tepuis" (Boone).

p. 54 "might seem counter-intuitive" (Rhodes).

p. 59 "The creative person" (Katz).

p. 60 "You can't use up creativity" (Angelou).

PART TWO: Maintain Momentum

Chapter 5 OPTIMIZE: Honor Your Workstyle

p. 68 "Listen to these Plotters" To see samples of the detailed plans and outlines of several famous writers, see Tara Brady's "Losing the Plot."

p. 68 "the easier the book is to write" ("Literary Birthday")

p. 68 "sturdy table of contents" (Silvia 114).

p. 68 "I'm a plotter" (Bowe).

p. 68 "best-selling English authors of all time" (L. Miller).

p. 68 "acute compositional rigor" (Wu).

p. 69 "Faulkner wrote the complete chapter" (Jones).

p. 69 "they don't know what they think" (Wallas 106).

p. 69 “I like to think of the book as being an adventure” (Morrell qtd. in Strawser).

p. 69 “The big benefit” (Lowrey).

p. 69 “you can’t plot tomorrow” (Bradbury).

p. 70 “This is what I wanna do” (“Eminem ‘got over writer’s block’”).

p. 70 “I have long since ceased to invent” (Tolkien 231).

p. 70 “I met a lot of things on the way” (Tolkien 216–17).

p. 72 “floating outline” (Sanderson).

p. 72 “[C. S. Lewis] was an internal processor” C. S. Lewis’s writing process sometimes took weeks; with other projects, it took years. There are projects he pondered for decades, trying to find the right form, tone, and approach. His extraordinary novel *Till We Have Faces*, conceived when he was in his teens and written when he was in his fifties, is but one example.

p. 73 “[C. S. Lewis] revised some of the same lines for decades.” In 2000, when an editor named Don W. King decided to collect Lewis’s poetry in one volume, he faced the daunting task of deciding which version of each poem should be considered authoritative: The original? The one that was published? Or the version that Lewis revised some ten or twenty years later? Emily Dickinson scholars ran into the same difficulty, especially since very few of her 1,800 poems were published during her lifetime.

p. 77 “enhance creativity by changing conditions in the environment” (Csikszentmihalyi 1).

p. 79 “Rituals are a good signal to your unconscious” (Lamott 117).

p. 79 “crave salty, crunchy foods” According to Dr. Hugh Humphery, “Crunchy foods lead to enhanced neural responses in areas of the brain that experience pleasantness and reward, increasing the sensation of well-being and secondarily reducing stress” (Humphery qtd. in Yazawa).

p. 80 “deep work” (MacNeil).

p. 80 “more than four hours without a break.” Mihaly Csikszentmihalyi celebrates the power of *flow*, those moments when you are in a state of complete immersion in an activity and completely lose track of time. In an interview with *Wired*, he explains, “The ego falls away. Time flies. Every action, movement, and thought follows inevitably from the previous one, like playing jazz. Your whole being is involved, and you're using your skills to the utmost” (Csikszentmihalyi qtd. in Geirland).

p. 80 “four or five hours a day” (Huxley).

p. 81 “2,000 words a day” (King qtd. in Viam, “Secret of Great Writers”).

p. 81 “three to four hours a day” (Fitzgerald qtd. in Viam, “How Many Words Should I Write?”).

p. 81 “I write every morning” (Munro qtd. in Simmonds).

p. 81 “I wake at 5 a.m.” (Trollope qtd. in Simmonds).

p. 81 “Every day I get up” (Stine).

p. 81 “I have two or three things” (Babauta).

p. 81 “Three focused hours” (Doran).

pp. 81–82 “Seeing lots of people” (Pulley).

Chapter 6 DRAFT: Write Fast!

p. 87 “Almost all good writing begins with terrible first efforts” (Lamott 25).

p. 87 “I’m simply shoveling sand into a box” (Hale).

p. 88 “get it right the first time” (Cormier qtd. in Silvey 150).

p. 91 “outracing the censors” (Murray, *Craft of Revision* 17–18).

pp. 91–92 “hidden in our minds” (Murray, *Craft of Revision* 51).

p. 94 “The voice of the oppressor” (Lamott 93).

p. 94 “Not one of them writes elegant first drafts” (Lamott 21).

p. 94 “You can’t edit a blank page” (Picoult).

p. 94 “hastily translated from Icelandic by a non-native speaker” (Silvia 76).

p. 94 “‘ugly babies’ of creativity” (Catmull 131).

p. 95 “you just get it down” (Lamott 25).

Chapter 7 PERSIST: Overcome Obstacles

p. 101 “no such thing as writer’s block” (Simon qtd. in Schultz).

p. 102 “the superpower of the 21st century” (Newport 14).

p. 104 “Always sticky notes” Visual processes are often very productive for me. You may be more drawn to auditory strategies (tape recordings, audiobooks, talking with a friend), or kinesthetic ones (jotting notes on index cards, or cutting pages into chunks and rearranging). If you haven’t investigated the various learning styles, I recommend you do a bit of research. You may find that varying your learning style helps you develop effective strategies for modifying your writing habits.

p. 104 “clicking mouse buttons” (Kleon 60).

pp. 104–5 “Touch Your Toes” (Provost 22).

p. 106 “NaNoWriMo.” Short for National Novel Writing Month, NaNoWriMo is a nonprofit best known for its yearly program in which participants attempt to write a 50,000 word manuscript in the month of November.

PART THREE: (Finally!) Get it Done

Chapter 8 REWORK: Review the Big Picture

p. 115 “First drafts are for learning” (Malamud).

pp. 116-117 “Revising is the radical process” Recommended books on revision include *The Anatomy of Story* by John Truby; *Scene & Structure* by Jack M. Bickham; *Plot &*

Structure by James Scott Bell; and *Good Prose: The Art of Nonfiction* by Tracy Kidder and Richard Todd. The gold standard text on the topic of revising your manuscript is *Developmental Editing* by Scott Norton.

p. 119 "a different part of our brain is engaged" (Hayes).

p. 119 "he put it in a drawer for a year" (Bradbury qtd. in Weller).

p. 120 "the patterns in our eye movement change" (Sharmin, Špakov, and Räihä).

p. 121 "Hit the print button" (Scanlan qtd. in Murray, *Craft of Revision* 173). Chip Scanlan continues to share important perspectives about the craft of writing at www.chipswritingles-sons.com/. His work is engaging, helpful, and motivating.

p. 124 "a reverse outline." Most people think of an outline as a planning tool, something you prepare before you start to write. A "reverse outline" simply means that you build the outline after you have already drafted the text itself. Outlining after you write can be a great way to assess your progress, clarify your message, check your sequencing, or simply get your mind back into the project so that you can make new progress.

p. 125 "I have two desks in my office" (Kleon 60–61).

pp. 126–27 "*Finding Nemo*" (Catmull 132–34).

p. 128 "give it proportional space" (Dillard, "Notes to Young Writers").

p. 129 "tighter, stronger, and more precise" (Zinsser 11).

p. 130 "say one thing" (Murray, *Craft of Revision* 46).

p. 130 "engaging their attention and anticipating their needs." Experienced writers get better and better at maintaining a focus on the needs of the reader, even in the earliest planning stages of a project. But too much consideration of your audience too soon in the process may silence the quirky, deep, powerful, meaningful message that is closest to your heart.

p. 131 "1,400-word article for a magazine" To read the full article, see Glyer, "Traveling through the Dark."

p. 132 "kill your darlings" (King 222).

p. 133 "Put it in a drawer" (Lewis *Collected Letters* 3:1108–9). C. S. Lewis offered this advice in a letter dated 14 December 1959 to a seventh-grade student named Thomasine, whose teacher had asked students to write to a well-known author for guidance on writing.

pp. 137–38 "stretched to my limit" Perceptive readers will be correct in guessing that for ten months, while I was drafting this book, I endured an endless parade of workmen as I completed a long-awaited kitchen remodel.

p. 139 "rewrote the ending…thirty-nine times" (Murray, *Craft of Revision* 253).

p. 139 "We could go on, revising this draft" (Murray, *Craft of Revision* 256).

Chapter 9 EDIT: Refine Your Style

p. 142 "To write is human, to edit is divine" (King 222).

p. 143 "help authors improve the impact of their prose." For an extended treatment of editing, see *Self-Editing for Fiction*

Writers by Browne and King, *The Elements of Style* by Strunk and White, *The Sense of Style: The Thinking Person's Guide to Writing in the 21st Century* by Steven Pinker, *Revision and Self-Editing for Publication* by James Scott Bell, *Dreyer's English: An Utterly Correct Guide to Clarity and Style* by Benjamin Dreyer, *Line by Line: How to Edit Your Own Writing* by Claire Kehrwald Cook, and *Editing Secrets of Best-Selling Authors* by Kathy Ide.

p. 144 "people forget 50% of what the doctor says" (Bodenheimer).

p. 144 "reading level is grade eight" (Hersh et al. 118).

p. 146 "olive-green blouse, and heels" Case in point: In the first draft of this chapter, I wrote this sentence this way: "Tomorrow, I'll dress for work in black slacks, an olive-green blouse, and heels." When my editor read it, she said, "Most readers don't use the word 'slacks' anymore. They won't know what that means." So I changed it.

p. 150 "write music" (Provost 60–61).

pp. 151–52 "It certainly helps if the stories are riveting" (Karr 36).

p. 152 "So now I teach" (Lamott xxvii).

p. 154 "Always write (and read) with the ear" (Lewis *Collected Letters* 3:1108).

p. 154 "If it doesn't sound nice, try again" (Lewis *Collected Letters* 3:1108).

p. 160 "leeches that infest the pond of prose" (Strunk and White 40).

p. 164 "Omit needless words." This three-word mantra has been made famous by Strunk and White in *The Elements of Style*. You'll find it quoted everywhere.

Chapter 10 PROOFREAD: Fix Mistakes

p. 166 "When speaking aloud, you punctuate constantly" (Baker).

p. 168 "this proofreading chapter is not intended as a comprehensive guide" For an in-depth guide to proofreading, we recommend *Proofreading Secrets of Best-Selling Authors* by Kathy Ide, *Eats, Shoots & Leaves* by Lynne Truss, *The Best Punctuation Book, Period* by June Casagrande, and *The Elements of Editing* by Arthur Plotnik. My all-time favorite writer's handbook is *A Writer's Reference* by Diana Hacker.

p. 168 "Our brain, trying to be helpful, fills in the gaps" (Stockton).

p. 171 "two countries divided by a common language" (Shaw qtd. in "Popular British Sayings").

p. 171 "British conventions" British spelling is used in England, Ireland, Northern Ireland, Scotland, and Wales. It is also used in Australia, New Zealand, India, Singapore, and South Africa. Canada uses a mix of British and American spellings and language conventions.

p. 174 "added to the dictionary" There are several websites that keep track of new words and identify "the word of the year." You can see a list of some of these here:

en.wikipedia.org/wiki/Word_of_the_year.

p. 174 "the use of the first-person in academic writing" The 1980s saw a big shift toward the use of more informal language in scholarly journals, including increased use of personal pronouns and personal stories. One notable example is "Frequency of Formal Errors in Current College Writing, or Ma and Pa Kettle Do Research," an influential 1988 article by Robert J. Connors and Andrea A. Lunsford, published in *College Composition and Communication*.

p. 175 "struggling with one specific rule or tendency." I have appreciated the work of Andrea A. Lunsford and Robert J. Connors in identifying the most common patterns of proofreading errors they found after researching and analyzing thousands of student essays written over several decades (Connors and Lunsford 395-409).

PART FOUR: WHAT'S NEXT?

Chapter 11 PUBLISH: Reach Your Readers

p. 182 "he also gained a new sense of his own story" (McAdams). Studies in neuroscience suggest that someone who can narrate the events of their own life is mentally healthier and more resilient than someone who cannot. It's even better if it is in writing. Someone who has done this is stronger mentally and emotionally than someone who had an easier life but hasn't found a way to tell their story.

p. 193 "the process of making information…available to the public" ("Publishing").

p. 195 "the actual act of writing — turns out to be the best part" (Lamott xxvi).

Chapter 12 THRIVE: Cultivate a More Creative Life

p. 198 “Blue Ridge Highway.” For images of this mural and more about the collaborative process that produced it, visit www.DianaGlyer.com/mural.

p. 199 “the right method for you” (Zinsser 5).

p. 202 “holding a chair at the thing and shouting ‘Simba!’” (Dillard, *The Writing Life* 52).

p. 202 “ write every day” King 153

p. 202 “drunk on writing” Bradbury xii

p. 202 “showing up daily regardless” Pressfield 100

p. 203 “routine is a better friend than inspiration” (Keyes 252).

pp. 203 “four hours a week” (Silvia 13).

p. 203 “five hundred words a day” (Goins).

p. 204 “I don’t want to ‘break the chain’” (Clear 196).

p. 204 “spend your time sitting down and moving your mittens” (Silvia 8).

p. 208 “a writer and a reader” I would argue that even when we are engaged with expressive writing, such as journaling or writing angsty poetry, we are writing for a reader (our future selves, our hurting selves, our stubborn selves) who needs to understand what we are going through. Sometimes, we are the one essential audience for what we write.

p. 208 “Has nobody got anything to read us?” (Glyer, *Bandersnatch*, 24)

p. 211 “designed to communicate face to face” (Drijvers and Holler).

p. 212 “set a very ambitious goal to get the first draft done quickly.” Completing a rough draft or a first draft is often too daunting for me. So, I call it a “zero draft.” No pressure. Just get something down.

p. 213 “gratefully receive this priceless gift” It is hard to over-emphasize how helpful it was to make use of every spare scrap of paper in those days. Tolkien composed one of the most famous lines in literature, “In a hole in the ground there lived a hobbit,” on a blank page of a School Certificate examination paper that he was grading in the summer of 1930 (Garth).

p. 215 “The writer is a person who writes” (Murray, *Essential* 74).

p. 216 “sit before a piece of paper” (“250 Quotes by Flannery O’Connor”).

p. 216 “She was a magnificent sitter” (Murray, *Essential* 76).

Bibliography

Nothing gives an author so great pleasure as to find his works respectfully quoted by others.
Benjamin Franklin

Angelou, Maya. *Conversations with Maya Angelou.* Edited by Jeffrey M. Elliot, University Press of Mississippi, 1989.

Babauta, Leo. "How to Create the Habit of Writing." *Write to Done: Unmissable Articles on Writing*, www.writetodone.com/habit-of-writing/.

Baker, Russell. "How to punctuate." *Editing Monks*, 11 Feb. 2006, www.editingmonks.blogspot.com/2006/02.

Bell, James Scott. *Plot & Structure: Techniques and Exercises for Crafting a Plot That Grips Readers from Start to Finish.* Writer's Digest Books, 2004.

---. *Revision and Self-Editing for Publication*. Writer's Digest Books, 2012.

Bickham, Jack M. *Scene & Structure*. Writer's Digest Books, 1999.

Bodenheimer, Thomas. "Teach-Back: A Simple Technique to Enhance Patients' Understanding." *Family Practice Management* 25, no. 4, July/Aug. 2018, pp. 20–22, American Academy of Family Physicians, www.aafp.org/pubs/fpm/issues/2018/0700/p20.html.

Boone, Christopher. "How Do Disney and Pixar Come Up with Those Ingenious Stories? Through Research & Development." *No Film School*, 9 Nov. 2016, www.nofilmschool.com/2016.
Bowe, Steph. "Author Interview: Nick Earls." 5 Feb. 2010, http://www.stephbowe.com.

Bradbury, Ray. *Zen in the Art of Writing: Releasing the Creative Genius Within You*. HarperCollins, 1990.

Brady, Tara. "Losing the Plot." *Daily Mail UK*, 19 May 2013. www.dailymail.co.uk.

Browne, Renni, and Dave King. *Self-Editing for Fiction Writers: How to Edit Yourself into Print*. 2nd ed., Harper Resource, 2004.

Burke, Kenneth. *The Philosophy of Literary Form*. University of California Press, 1974.

Cameron, Julia. "Morning Pages." *The Artist's Way*, 19 Apr. 2017, www.juliacameronlive.com/2017.

Casagrande, June. *The Best Punctuation Book, Period*. Ten Speed Press, 2014.

Catmull, Ed, and Amy Wallace. *Creativity, Inc.: Overcoming the Unseen Forces That Stand in the Way of True Inspiration*. Random House, 2014.

Chee, Alexander. "Annie Dillard and the Writing Life." *The Morning News*, 16 Oct. 2009, themorningnews.org/article/annie-dillard-and-the-writing-life.

Chekhov, Anton. *The Unknown Chekhov: Stories and Other Writings Hitherto Untranslated.* Translated, edited, and introduced by Avrahm Yarmolinsky. Noonday Press, 1954.

Cirillo, Francesco. *The Pomodoro Technique: The Acclaimed Time-Management System That Has Transformed How We Work.* Currency, 2018.

Clear, James. *Atomic Habits: An Easy & Proven Way to Build Good Habits & Break Bad Ones.* Avery, 2018.

Cook, Claire Kehrwald. *Line by Line: How to Edit Your Own Writing.* Collins Reference, 1985.

Csikszentmihalyi, Mihaly. *Creativity: Flow and the Psychology of Discovery and Invention.* HarperCollins, 1996.

Comer, John Mark. *Practicing the Way: Be with Jesus, Become Like Him, Do as He Did.* WaterBrook, 2024.

Connors, Robert J., and Andrea Lunsford. "Frequency of Formal Errors in Current College Writing, or Ma and Pa Kettle Do Research." *College Composition and Communication, vol.* 39, no. 4, 1 Dec. 1988, pp. 395–409.

Currey, Mason. "The Creatives: The Daily Ritual of Haruki Murakami." *The Guardian*, 27 March 2009, www.theguardian.com/books/2009/mar/27/murakami-what-talk-about-running.

Didion, Joan. "Why I Write." *The New York Times Magazine*, 5 Dec. 1976, www.nytimes.com/1976/12/05/archives/why-i-write-why-i-write.html.

Dillard, Annie. "Notes to Young Writers." *Image Journal*, no. 16, www.imagejournal.org/article/notes-for-young-writers/.

---. *The Writing Life*. Harper, 2009.

Doran, Mark Douglas. "Why 3 Hours Is Enough Time in a Day to Write a Novel." *Mark Douglas Doran*, 25 Nov. 2021, www.markdouglasdoran.com/3-hours-enough-time-write-novel/.

Drijvers, Linda and Judith Holler. "Face-to-face Spatial Orientation Fine-tunes the Brain for Neurocognitive Processing in Conversation." *iScience,* vol. 25, no. 11, 2022, www.pubmed.ncbi.nlm.nih.gov/36388995/.

Dreyer, Benjamin. *Dreyer's English: An Utterly Correct Guide to Clarity and Style*. Random House, 2019.

Einstein, Bob. Response to "Where do you get your ideas from?" *Norm Macdonald Live*, YouTube, uploaded by "I'm not Norm," 2021, www.youtube.com/watch?v=MKnIlrZVtWY.

Elbow, Peter. *Writing with Power: Techniques for Mastering the Writing Process*. Oxford University Press, 1998.

"Eminem 'got over writer's block.'" Interview by BBC Newsbeat, *BBC News*, 20 May 2009, news.bbc.co.uk/newsbeat/hi/music/newsid_8058000/8058163.stm.

Frost, Robert. "The Road Not Taken." *Poetry Foundation, 1915,* www.poetryfoundation.org/poems/44272.

Gaiman, Neil. "Neil Gaiman on Libraries." *The Indianapolis Public Library,* 16 Apr. 2010, www.youtube.com/watch?v=uH-sR1uCQ6g.

Garth, John. "Testing Time for Tolkien, the Inklings and the T.C.B.S." https://johngarth.wordpress.com/2021/06/12/testing-time.

Geirland, John. "Go With the Flow." *Wired*, Sept. 1996, www.wired.com/1996/09/czik/.

Glyer, Diana Pavlac. *Bandersnatch: C. S. Lewis, J. R. R. Tolkien, and the Creative Collaboration of the Inklings*. Kent State University Press, 2015.

---. "Blog." www.dianaglyer.com/home.

---. *The Company They Keep: C. S. Lewis and J. R. R. Tolkien as Writers in Community.* Kent State University Press, 2007.

---. *The Major and the Missionary: The Letters of Warren Hamilton Lewis and Blanche Biggs.* Rabbit Room Press, 2023.

---. "Traveling Through the Dark." A*PU Life*, Azusa Pacific University, 15 Jan. 2025, www.apu.edu/articles/traveling-through-the-dark/.

Goins, Jeff. "The Secret to Developing a Regular Writing Habit: 500 Words a Day." *Medium,* 5 Jan. 2016, www.medium.com/@jeffgoins/the-secret-to-developing-a-regular-writing-habit.

Hacker, Diana. *A Writer's Reference*. Bedford/St. Martin's, 2017.

Haig, Matt. "Why I Love My Library." *The Guardian,* 8 Feb. 2013, www.theguardian.com/childrens-books-site/2013.

Hale, Shannon [@haleshannon]. "When writing a first draft…." X, 27 Aug. 2015, 7:27 a.m., x.com/haleshannon/status/636907891379736576.

Harris, Joseph. *Rewriting: How To Do Things with Texts*. University Press of Colorado, 2006.

Hayes, John R. "A New Framework for Understanding Cognition and Affect in Writing." *The Science of Writing: Theories, Methods, Individual Differences, and Applications*, edited by Charles A. MacArthur, Steve Graham, and Jill Fitzgerald, Lawrence Erlbaum Associates, 2006, pp. 1–27.

Heller, Joseph. *Catch-22*. Simon & Schuster, 1961.

Henry, Patti Callahan, and Mary Kay Andrews, hosts. "The Anatomy of Genres with John Truby." *Friends & Fiction*, season 2, episode 49, 1 Dec. 2022, www.podcasts.apple.com/us/podcast/wb-s2e49.

Hersh, Lauren, et al. "Health Literacy in Primary Care Practice." *American Family Physician*, vol. 92, no. 2, 2015, www.nursing.jhu.edu/wp-content/uploads/2023/02/Health-Literacy-in-Primary-Care-Practice.pdf.

Hinckley, Gordon B. "Called to Serve." *Ensign*, Nov. 1987. www.churchofjesuschrist.org/.

"History of Wikipedia." *Wikipedia*, en.wikipedia.org/wiki/History of Wikipedia.

The Hobbit: An Unexpected Journey. Directed by Peter Jackson, performances by Ian McKellen, Martin Freeman, and Richard Armitage, Warner Bros. Pictures / New Line Cinema, 2012.

"How Do You Get Your Ideas?" Authors' Answers to the Eternal Question. *Book Riot*, 24 Mar. 2022, www.bookriot.com/ how-do-you-get-your-ideas/.

Huxley, Aldous. "The Art of Fiction No. 24." Interview by George Wickes and Raymond Fraser. *The Paris Review*, no. 24, Spring 1960, www.theparisreview.org/interviews/4698/the-art-of-fiction-no-24-aldous-huxley.

Ide, Kathy. *Editing Secrets of Best-Selling Authors*. Lighthouse Publishing of the Carolinas, 2020.

---. *Proofreading Secrets of Best-Selling Authors*. Lighthouse Publishing of the Carolinas, 2013.

Jefferson, Thomas. Letter to John Minor. 30 Aug. 1814. Founders Online, National Archives, founders.archives.gov/ documents/Jefferson/03-07-02-0455.

Jones, Josh. "William Faulkner Outlines on His Office Wall the Plot of His Pulitzer Prize Winning Novel, *A Fable* (1954)." *Open Culture*, 12 Feb. 2015, www.openculture.com/2015/02/ william-faulkner-outlines-on-his-office-wall-the-plot-of-a-fable.html.

Karr, Mary. *The Art of Memoir.* Harper, 2015.

Katz, Charlie. "Creativity Is Never Saying No." *Bitbean*, www.bitbean.com/blog/creativity-never-saying-no/.

Kent, Louise Andrews. *Mrs. Appleyard's Kitchen*. Houghton Mifflin, 1942.

Keyes, Ralph. *The Courage to Write: How Writers Transcend Fear*. Henry Holt and Co., 1995.

Kidder, Tracy, and Richard Todd. *Good Prose: The Art of Nonfiction*. Random House, 2013.

King, Don W., editor. *The Collected Poems of C. S. Lewis: A Critical Edition*. Kent State University Press, 2020.

King, Stephen. *On Writing: A Memoir of the Craft*. Scribner, 2000.

Klein, Annika Barranti. "'How Do You Get Your Ideas?' Authors' Answers to Their Most Common Question." *Book Riot*. https://bookriot.com/how-do-you-get-your-ideas/. 2022.

Kleon, Austin. *Steal Like an Artist*. Workman Publishing, 2012.

Lamott, Anne. *Bird by Bird: Some Instructions on Writing and Life*. Knopf Doubleday, 1995.

Lee, Christine Hyung-Oak. "The best of times, the worst of times, and the work." 17 Jan. 2015, http://xtinehlee.com.

Leonard, Elmore. "Easy on the Adverbs, Exclamation Points and Especially Hooptedoodle." *The New York Times*, 16 July 2001, www.nytimes.com/2001/07/16.

Lewis, C. S. *The Collected Letters of C. S. Lewis*. Vol. 3, edited by Walter Hooper, HarperOne, 2007.

---. *Till We Have Faces: A Myth Retold*. Harcourt Brace, 1980.

"Literary Birthday." *Writers Write,* 8 Feb. 2013, www.writerswrite.co.za/literary-birthday-8-february-john-grisham.

London, Jack. "Getting into Print." *No Mentor But Myself: Jack London on Writing and Writers*, edited by Dale L. Walker and Jeanne Campbell Reesman, Stanford UP, 1999.

Lowrey, Sassafras. "Pantser or Planner?" *Publishers Weekly*, 8 Jan. 2021, www.publishersweekly.com/pw/by-topic/authors/pw-select/article/85267-pantser-or-planner.html.

Macrorie, Ken. *The I-Search Paper.* Heinemann, 1988.

MacNeil, Caeleigh. "What Is Deep Work? 7 Ways to Boost Your Concentration." *Asana*, 29 Oct. 2022.

Malamud, Bernard. "The Art of Fiction No. 52." Interview by Daniel Stern. *The Paris Review*, no. 52, Spring 1973, www.theparisreview.org/interviews/3869/the-art-of-fiction-no-52-bernard-malamud.

McAdams, Dan P., and Kate C. McLean. "Narrative Identity." *Current Directions in Psychological Science*, vol. 22, no. 3, 2013, pp. 233–38.

McPhee, John. "Progression." *The New Yorker*, 14 Nov. 2011, www.newyorker.com/magazine/2011/11/14/progression.

Miller, John J. "Kurt Vonnegut: 16 Rules for Writing Fiction." *Book Marketing Bestsellers*, bookmarketingbestsellers.com/kurt-vonnegut.

Miller, Laura. "How James Patterson Became the World's Best-selling Author." *The New Yorker,* June 2022, www.newyorker.com/magazine/2022/06/20.

Miranda, Lin-Manuel. "The World Was Wide Enough." *Hamilton* (Original Broadway Cast Recording), Atlantic 551093-2, 2015, compact disc.

Mozart, Wolfgang Amadeus. "Sonata Facile." *Piano Sonata No. 16 in C Major, K 545*, 1805.

Murray, Donald M. *The Craft of Revision.* 5th edition. Heinle Cengage Learning, 2004.

---. *The Essential Don Murray: Lessons from America's Greatest Writing Teacher*. Edited by Thomas Newkirk and Lisa C. Miller, Boynton/Cook, 2009.

Nelson, Dean. *Talk to Me: How to Ask Better Questions, Get Better Answers, and Interview Anyone Like a Pro*. Harper Perennial, 2019.

Newport, Cal. *Deep Work: Rules for Focused Success in a Distracted World.* Grand Central Publishing, 2016.

Norton, Scott. *Developmental Editing: A Handbook for Freelancers, Authors, and Publishers*. University of Chicago Press, 2023.

Palmer, Geoff. "A Writing Exercise Courtesy of Harlan Ellison." *Geoff Palmer*, 9 July 2018, www.geoffpalmer.co.nz/a-little-writing-exercise.

Picoult, Jodi. "Jodi Picoult: You Can't Edit a Blank Page." *NPR*, 22 Nov. 2006, www.npr.org/2006/11/22/6524058/jodi-picoult-you-cant-edit-a-blank-page.

Pinker, Steven. *The Sense of Style: The Thinking Person's Guide to Writing in the 21st Century*. Penguin Books, 2015.

Plotnik, Arthur. *The Elements of Editing: A Modern Guide for Editors and Journalists*. Collier Macmillan, 1984.

Popova, Maria. "Order to the Chaos of Life: Isabel Allende on Writing." *The Marginalian*, 18 Feb. 2013, www.themarginalian.org/2013/02/18/isabel-allende-on-writing/.

"Popular British Sayings." *Reader's Digest*, www.rd.com/list/popular-british-sayings/.

Pressfield, Steven. *The War of Art: Break Through the Blocks and Win Your Inner Creative Battles.* Black Irish Entertainment LLC, 2019.

Provost, Gary. *100 Ways to Improve Your Writing*. Berkley, 1985.

"Publishing." *Wikipedia,* www.en.wikipedia.org/wiki/publishing.

Pulley, Natasha. *China Daily*, 26 July 2019, www.chinadaily.com.cn/hkedition/2019.

Rhodes, Margaret. "Perfecting Pixar's Movies Takes a Crazy Amount of Research." *Wired,* 9 Oct. 2015, www.wired.com/2015/10/perfecting-pixars-movies-takes-crazy-amount-research/.

Rowan, Lisa. "Pantser or Planner? What Your Writing Style Says About You." *The Write Life*, 14 Nov. 2017, www.thewritelife.com/what-is-your-writing-style/.

Salesses, Matthew. *Craft in the Real World: Rethinking Fiction Writing and Workshopping*. Catapult, 2021.

Sanderson, Brandon. "Can You Go into Depth About Outlining?" *Brandon Sanderson*, 2018, www.faq.brandon-sanderson.com/knowledge-base/can-you-go-into-depth-about-outlining/.

Santoli, Lorraine. "The Top Reason People Never Finish Writing Their Book." *The Synergy Whisperer*, 20 Oct. 2015, www.thesynergyexpert.com/2015/10/20.

Scanlan, Chip. *Chip on Your Shoulder*, www.chipswriting lessons.com/.

Schultz, Jennifer. "Dealing With Writer's Block." *Lumivero*, 10 Feb. 2023, www.lumivero.com/resources/dealing-with-writers.

Sharmin, Selina, Oleg Špakov, and Kari-Jouko Räihä. "The Effect of Different Text Presentation Formats on Eye Movement Metrics in Reading." *Journal of Eye Movement Research*, vol. 5, no. 3, 2012, pp. 1–9. doi.org/10.16910/jemr.5.3.3.

Silvia, Paul J. *How to Write a Lot: A Practical Guide to Productive Academic Writing*. American Psychological Association, 2007.

Silvey, Anita. "An Interview with Robert Cormier." *The Horn Book Magazine*, vol. 61, no. 2, Mar./Apr. 1985, pp. 145–55.

Simmonds, Alex. "Daily Habits & Writing Routines of 21 Famous Authors." *ProWritingAid*, 2 May 2022, www.prowrit-ingaid.com/writing-routines-famous-authors.

Stine, R. L. "R. L. Stine on Writing Goosebumps." *The Verge*, 28 April 2021.

Stockton, Nick. "What's Up with That: Why It's So Hard to Catch Your Own Typos." *Wired*, 12 Aug. 2014, www.wired.com/2014/08/wuwt-typos/.

Strawser, Jessica. "David Morrell & Ken Follett Talk About Writing." *Writer's Digest*, 8 Oct. 2010, www.writersdigest.com/improve-my-writing/follett-morrell.

Strunk, William, Jr., and E. B. White. *The Elements of Style*. 4th ed., Pearson, 2000.

Temple, Emily. "12 Contemporary Writers on How They Revise." *Literary Hub*, 10 Jan. 2017, www.lithub.com/12-contemporary-writers.

Tolkien, J. R. R. *The Letters of J. R. R. Tolkien*. Edited by Humphrey Carpenter with the assistance of Christopher Tolkien. Houghton Mifflin Company, 2000.

Trott, Dave. "Really Creative People." *DaveTrott.co.uk*, 12 Dec. 2008, davetrott.co.uk/2008/12/really-creative-people.

Truby, John. *The Anatomy of Genres: How Story Forms Explain the Way the World Works*. Picador Paper, 2022.

Truss, Lynne. *Eats, Shoots & Leaves: The Zero Tolerance Approach to Punctuation*. Avery, 2006.

Twain, Mark. Letter to D. W. Bowser. 20 Mar. 1880. *Mark Twain Project Online,* University of California, www.marktwainproject.org/.

"250 Quotes by Flannery O'Connor." *AZ Quotes*, www.azquotes.com/author/.

Viam. “How Many Words Should I Write a Day to Be a Good Writer?” *Medium,* 2 March 2023, www.medium.com /@viam_/how-many-words-should-i-write.

---. “The Secret of Great Writers: Daily Word Count.” *Medium*, 24 Nov. 2023, www.medium.com/@viam_/the-secret-of-great-writers.

Vonnegut, Kurt. *Bagombo Snuff Box: Uncollected Short Fiction*. G. P. Putnam’s Sons, 1999.

---. *Palm Sunday: An Autobiographical Collage*. Delacorte Press, 1981.

Wallas, Graham. *The Art of Thought.* Solis Press, 1926.

Weller, Sam. “Ray Bradbury, The Art of Fiction No. 203.” *The Paris Review*, no. 203, Spring 2010, www.theparisreview.org/interviews/6012.

Wu, Professor. “Compositional Rigour: Joseph Heller’s Organisational Chart for ‘*Catch-22*.’” *Nothing in the Rulebook*, 9 Oct. 2019, www.nothingintherulebook.com/2019.

Yazawa, Maki. “Why People Are *So* in Love with Crunchy Food According to a Gastrophysicist and Psychiatrist.” *Well+Good*, 26 Nov. 2022, www.wellandgood.com/why-i-crave-crunchy-food/.

Zinsser, William. *On Writing Well*. HarperCollins, 2012.

About the Authors

Diana Pavlac Glyer has been teaching writing for decades, and she loves what she does. An award-winning author and sought-after speaker, she has published in multiple genres, including fiction, poetry, play scripts, scholarly articles, and inspirational literature. She is best known for her best-selling book *Bandersnatch: C. S. Lewis, J. R. R. Tolkien, and the Creative Collaboration of the Inklings*. Dr. Glyer earned her PhD in Composition Studies and has experience directing a writing center, presenting writing workshops, and overseeing writing programs at the high school and college levels. She teaches full-time in the Honors College at Azusa Pacific University in Southern California, where she lives in a little yellow house and, whenever she gets the chance, goes hiking in the San Gabriel Mountains with two scruffy terriers named Jackson McCatterson and Jellybean. To learn more, visit DianaGlyer.com.

Abigail Stone is a writer, editor, and book coach driven by a deep joy in helping writers shape words that matter. From the Azusa Pacific University Writing Center to publishing houses such as Indigo River Publishing and Berry Powell Press, she has contributed to dozens of published books and guided hundreds of writers from first concepts to finished manuscripts. She has continued to develop her craft through the Editorial Freelancers Association and the UCLA Extension program and serves as an active member of the Independent Book Publishers Association. Abigail lives in Pasadena, CA, where she enjoys figure skating and library hauls. Connect with her at abigailstonebooks.com.

Note From the Publisher

Authors are at the heart of Berry Powell Press. As a publishing house centered on supporting authors as they bring their vision to life, BPP probably offers no greater service than putting this essential information in the hands of writers struggling to get their ideas and stories onto the page.

Write Like You Mean It is one-of-a-kind among the many books written for writers by writers. Most offer a reflection of a single author from their personal perspective and writing process. But this team of authors, Dr. Diana Pavlac Glyer and Abigail Stone, bring an unmatched perspective that will set this book apart.

The authors draw from a breadth of education and study, the reach of extensive research, a depth of personal writing, publishing, and editorial experience, and years of book coaching and classroom instruction that is extremely difficult to match. This book was crafted with attention to detail and a love of the art of writing that glows from its pages.

It is a great honor to be included in this project, and we are confident that this book will reach thousands, if not millions, of writers and change the trajectory of their novels, essays, transformational guidance, and all the forms that writing can take.

Visit our website at www.berrypowellpress.com

Berry Powell Press is a hybrid publishing house founded by Carmen Renee Berry, a New York Times bestselling author. We publish authors with transformational perspectives on timely personal and societal challenges. BPP provides our authors with in-depth mentorship and collaborative assistance to create life-changing books. Additionally, we help them build book-based businesses that can reach the widest possible audience. BPP publishes fiction and non-fiction for adults and children.

www.ingramcontent.com/pod-product-compliance
Lightning Source LLC
LaVergne TN
LVHW010645110826
845149LV00014B/2960